THE SPANISH RIDING SCHOOL in Vienna:

Home of Equestrian Art

by General Decarpentry

Translated to English by E. Schmit-Jensen

AND

PIAFFE AND PASSAGE:

Preparation for Dressage Tests

by General Decarpentry

Translated to English by Patricia Galvin

Edited by Richard F. Williams

© Xenophon Press 2013

Title: *The Spanish Riding School in Vienna* and *Piaffe and Passage*
   by General Decarpentry
Copyright © 2013 by Xenophon Press LLC

Edited by Richard F. Williams
Cover design by Naia Poyer.

All rights reserved. No part of this work may be reproduced or transmitted in any form or by any means, electronic or mechanical, including photocopying, or by any information storage or retrieval system except by written permission from the publisher.

Published by

Xenophon Press LLC,

7518 Bayside Road,

Franktown, Virginia 23354-2106, U.S.A.

ISBN-10   0-933316-31-3
ISBN-13   978-0-933316-31-7

"The Spanish Riding School in Vienna: Home of the Art of Riding in Peril" first published in September 1947. J. A. Allen copyright 2nd quarter 1947. Translated by E. Schmit-Jensen.

"Piaffer and Passage" published & copyrighted by John Howell Books, 1961. Limited Edition.
"Piaffer and Passage" published and copyrighted by J.A. Allen, 1965.
"Piaffer and Passage" published and copyrighted by Arco Publishing, 1975. ISBN: 0668036761
"Piaffer and Passage" published and copyrighted Half-Halt Press, 1998. ISBN: 978-0939481514

TABLE OF CONTENTS:

About the Xenophon Press Edition i

THE SPANISH RIDING SCHOOL IN VIENNA

Introduction to the Xenophon Press Edition by Andreas Hausberger iv
Foreword III
History of the School 1
The Objective of the Riding School 4
The Staff of the Riding School 7
Exhibition of Riding Masters 8
The Lippizaner 9
The Riding School 12
The Exhibitions 15
The Principles of the Method of Training 17
The Method of Training 19
Dressage 23
Work "on the Hand" 24
Work "on the Long Reins" 27
Work in the Pillars 29
The *Haute École* 32
The School Canter 40
The School Jumps 42
Lindenbauer: Riding-Master-in-Chief 53
Program of a Gala Exhibition 55
Explanation of the Program 58

PIAFFE AND PASSAGE

Preface to the Xenophon Press Edition by J. P. Giacomini 65
Note on the Translation by Patricia Galvin 67
Preface by Colonel Pierre Danloux 69
Introduction 71
PART I : PIAFFE AND PASSAGE 73

The Suitable Order in Which to Begin These Two Airs 73
When to Begin the Training of the Piaffe 75
How to Prepare for the Piaffe 77
How to Begin the Piaffe 81
Developing the Piaffe 83
Raising the Forelegs 85
Developing the Scope of the Movement 89

PART II: DEVELOPMENT OF THE PIAFFE 91
Rectifying the General Position by Raising the Forehand 93
Developing the Action of the Forelegs 97

PART III: THE PASSAGE 103
Going to Passage from Piaffe 107
Passage Obtained from the Trot 113

BIBLIOGRAPHICAL NOTE 119

GENERAL DECARPENTRY 121

ABOUT THE XENOPHON PRESS EDITION

This book, the combination of two of Albert Decarpentry's works: *The Spanish Riding School in Vienna:home of equestrian art in peril* and *Piaffer and Passage: preparation for dressage tests,* represent Xenophon Press' commitment to preserving classical equestrian literature in the English language. These two books were first published as folios, in a large format for easy viewing of the many photographs. *Spanish Riding School* was written at a time when the future of the School was uncertain. It was a veritable call to arms to save the great school. Xenophon Press is passionate about preserving not only the literature, but also about raising awareness of the important work of the very few great equestrian schools remaining today. Our times are not dissimilar from the time when Decarpentry wrote his plea. Instability, economic changes, war and other varriables test the viability of these precious sanctuaries of classical horsemanship.

In Pierre Danloux's Preface to the first edition of *Piaffe and Passage*, he states that it comes at the right time (August 1932) to help riders prepare for up-coming Olympic Grand Prix tests. This pair of movements, the transitions between them, and the order of development have always challenged riders in search of excellence. *Piaffe and Passage* holds hidden secrets and insights from a twentieth century expert. We will all benefit from its contents. We returned to the original 1931 pictorial layout of *Piaffe and Passage* and enlarged and clarified the original photographs. While Patricia Galvin's translation served generations of English-speaking riders, there was room for better definitions of the French terms. Some of these, like *mise en main* and *rassembler,* were translated previously as "balance in the hand" and "gathering," respectively. While these vague English terms may have sufficed previously, we felt that some definitions and explanations were ambiguous. Returning to the original 1931 French manuscript, we clarify General Decarpentry's original usage of terms and intent. In some cases we have made corrections or additional notes, which are either held in hard brackets [ ] or footnoted. In these cases, we have done so in order to faithfully represent the original French meaning. This edition includes some detailed historical quotes and explanations provided by J. P. Giacomini.

We hope you benefit from the treasury of nuance contained herein.

-Richard F. Williams and Frances A. Williams
Xenophon Press

Xenophon Press Library

30 Years with Master Nuno Oliveira, Michel Henriquet 2011
A Rider's Survival From Tyranny, Charles de Kunffy 2012
Another Horsemanship, Jean-Claude Racinet, 1994
Art of the Lusitano, Pedro Yglesias de Oliveira 2012
Baucher and His School, General Decarpentry 2011
Dressage in the French Tradition, Dom Diogo de Bragança 2011
École de Cavalerie Part II (School of Horsemanship),
    François Robichon de la Guérinière 1992
François Baucher, The Man and His Method, Hilda Nelson 2013
From the Real Picaria of the 18th Century to the Portuguese School of
    Equestrian Art, Yglesias de Oliverira and da Costa 2012
Gymnastic Exercises for Horses Volume II, Eleanor Russell 2013
Healing Hands, Dominique Giniaux, DVM 1998
Methodical Dressage of the Riding Horse, and Dressage of the Outdoor
    Horse, Faverot de Kerbrech 2010
Racinet Explains Baucher, Jean-Claude Racinet 1997
The Écuyère of the Nineteenth Century in the Circus, Hilda Nelson 2001
The Ethics and Passions of Dressage, Expanded Edition,
    Charles de Kunffy 2013
The Gymnasium of the Horse, Gustav Steinbrecht 2011
The Handbook of Jumping Essentials,
    François Lemaire de Ruffieu 1997
The Legacy of Master Nuno Oliveira, Stephanie Millham 2013
The Maneige Royal, Antoine de Pluvinel 2010
The Spanish Riding School in Vienna and Piaffe and Passage,
    General Decarpentry 2013
The Wisdom of Master Nuno Oliveira, Antoine de Coux 2012
Total Horsemanship, Jean-Claude Racinet 1999
What the Horses Have Told Me, Dominique Giniaux, DVM 1996

Available at **www.XenophonPress.com**

The Spanish Riding School in Vienna

by **General Decarpentry**
Translated by E. Schmit-Jensen

XENOPHON PRESS

INTRODUCTION TO THE XENOPHON PRESS EDITION

The Spanish Riding School in Vienna is the only riding institute in the world that has been practicing classical riding in its purest form for more than 440 years. The means of transmitting knowledge has been primarily verbal for centuries. Classical riding practiced since ancient times, rediscovered in Italy, continued in Spain and England, grown to its fullest potential in France, and still today at home at the Spanish Riding School in Vienna is a form of riding that has flourished everywhere that man saw horses as creatures of equal worth. Classical riding does not belong to any one particular nation or people, regardless of who is guarding the tradition at any given time. While the Spanish Riding School guards this tradition with special care in our present time, this institution still sees in this only a responsibility – to the whole world.

If you question the contribution the Spanish Riding School makes, at a time when man can go to the moon, and in the not so distant future to mars, the answer is: art, the second answer: breeding. Horse and rider are melded together into an artistic personality, and the nobility of the art is interconnected with the nobility of the breed: an enhancement that does not exhaust itself in a moment, but rather remains beholden to the future and the past. That is how the circle is completed. A stallion, who is highly celebrated in the school, returns to the stud farm to pass on his nobility, power and talent to make room for a younger stallion at the school. The people who work at the school are subject to the same law; they are all links in a long chain that consists of all those who passed this treasure on into devoted hands. Our task is to maintain this inheritance and pass it on to a younger generation unspoiled.

Both works in this book are milestones in the history of classical riding and the Spanish Riding School. Thanks to Xenophon Press, these works will not be forgotten and will give the modern rider cause to reflect on many things in a critical way.

-Andreas Hausberger,
Chief Rider, The Spanish Riding School
Vienna, February 2013

Max von Weyrother*

"As far as the art of riding is concerned all nations have their particular rules and principles which vary more or less; what one nation considers good, another considers bad. The fashion and a sort of "bon ton" have caused the introduction of certain maxims which are distinguishable as the fruits of frivolity and ridicule; they are the products of vanity and are maintained out of vanity. In order to correct oneself it is necessary to travel a lot, to compare and sort out things and to possess great love of knowledge as well as good judgment."

*Adam von Weyrother**
Riding Master at the Austrian Court
1789

*The Weyrother family has produced four famous Riding Masters, one of whom, Antoine von Weyrother, was Riding Master-in-Chief at the Equestrian Academy at Nancy, Lorraine, in 1757.

FOREWORD

The first and most famous riding academy of modern times was founded at Versailles in 1680. A little more than a century later, it was closed during the French Revolution, re-opened in 1816, and finally closed its doors permanently in 1830.

The Spanish Riding School in Vienna was founded some forty years after the one in Versailles, more or less a replica and soon emulating the latter. More favorable circumstances enabled the Vienna Academy to survive all the storms in the European sky. Neither wars nor revolutions have interrupted its activities and its radiance over Central Europe has never waned.

Although its methods, which have remained the same for two centuries, admit to certain characteristic practices, its principles are the same as those of the Versailles Academy and it has never ceased adhering to François Robichon de la Guérinière and his *École de Cavalerie* [*School of Horsemanship Part II,* Xenophon Press 1992, 2013] which is recognized as "The Equestrian Bible."

The Riding Academy[1] was saved from the disaster following the fall of the Austro-Hungarian Empire mainly through the devotion of its Director, Count van der Straten, who, in order to prevent the dispersion of the personnel and horses, did not hesitate to spend his private fortune, and to maintain them until the new government took over the responsibility.

Now after a second disaster has befallen Austria[2], will the Riding Academy again be able to find a savior? Will this last conservatory of the Art of Equitation escape disaster?

No artist, no horseman of any nationality could remain indifferent to the risk of such an irreparable loss, but the French are particularly interested in the salvation of an institution which so faithfully adheres to the principles of the French School of the eighteenth century.

The Cavalry Riding School at Saumur has preserved part of the heritage of the Versailles School, namely the part applicable to "military" equitation, and perhaps a little more. But what will remain of this, now that the role

---

1   Spanish Riding School in Vienna
2   The Second World War

of the horse in the Army has been reduced to insignificance?

Regardless, among each of the Allied Nations, the Viennese zone where the Spanish Riding School resides should undoubtedly be able to depend on the support of the enlightened authority.

But doesn't France have the duty and the right to take an interest, more than any other nation, in the present and future of the last temple of Equestrian Art which has shone so brightly, and for so many centuries?

Thanks to General PATTON, who made a glorious name for himself on both sides of the Rhine, the Riding School in Vienna has been restored to its proper purpose.

General PATTON, an old pupil of Saumur and a keen and fine horseman, has rendered a great service in arranging the restoration of the temple which for two hundred years has been dedicated to the cult of the Art of Equitation.

The fatal accident[3] which claimed the life of General PATTON has deprived the Riding School of a badly needed supporter. Perhaps the Federation Equestre Internationale [F.E.I.], *through the culture committee of the U.N.O., could help this unique institution to regain its long established fame!*

P.S.   15th September, 1946.

Events have moved faster than the printing of this album. The Riding masters and Lippizaners have not returned to the Riding School in Vienna. When the fighting approached Vienna in 1945 they moved out of danger first to Ried and then to Wels, their present temporary quarters in the American zone — is fortunately on the right side of the "Iron curtain." Furthermore, the fear concerning the future of the Manège of the Saumur School expressed in the above is unfounded. The re-established Cadre Noir has just given its first gala-performance at St. Cloud. This renaissance is due to General DE LATTRE DE TASSIGNY.

May I, as his old Écuyer, express sincere and respectful gratitude on behalf of all the horsemen of France!

---

3   On December 9, 1945, Patton was severely injured in a motor vehicle accident, and died subsequently from a pulmonary embolism on December 21, 1945.

HISTORY OF THE SCHOOL

The famous Riding School in Vienna was founded by the Emperor Charles VI in 1729, but its origin traces back to the middle of the 16th century when "Spanish *Manège*" was in existence within the precincts of the Imperial Palace.

The denomination of "Spanish" still attached to the Riding School owes itself to the Spanish breed of horses which has always been used there.

Maximilian von Weyrother
(1818-1832)

Hans Meixner
(1898-1915)

It is difficult to reconstitute the history of the Riding School as only very few documents and dates are available. It would appear that one of the first Riding Masters-in-Chief was the Count von Regenthal. His most famous successor in the 19th century was Maximilian von Weyrother.

One of the most brilliant periods in the history of the Riding School was from 1865 to 1887 while Niedermayer was in charge. It was during this period, after the Franco-German war in 1870, that General L'Hotte spent a long time in Vienna preparing the French Manual of Cavalry Training of 1876. He was followed by Franz Gebhard, Hans Meixner (until 1915), Mauritius Herold, Zrust, Pollack and Lindenbauer, the latter being the Riding Master-in-Chief at the time of the writing of this work [1947].

**Frantz Gebhardt
(1887-1898)**

**Riding-Master-in-Chief Lindenbauer
(1919-1950)**

THE OBJECTIVE OF THE RIDING SCHOOL

The objective of the Spanish Riding School is expressly the conservation of the art of equitation in its most advanced state, the *Haute École*, in accordance with the tradition of the old Masters of the 18th century.

In order to fulfill this mission, the School always has some scholars in training to fill the position of Riding Masters when vacancies occur. Secondly, the school selects a number of young stallions from their particular stud farm, according to their suitability for the high school airs. These Lippizan horses, mainly descendants of Spanish foundation stock, are transferred every year to the Riding School in order to undergo systematic schooling; this

**Major Rodriguez
(Mexican Army)**

annual selection process has gone on for over two hundred years.

In the past, in addition to the scholars, the Riding School used to only admit as pupils Court officials, Imperial dignitaries and a few Army officers. Later, it was opened to foreign Army officers and selected civilians.

In the 19th century, the two most famous Riding Schools of old Germany, namely those at Hannover and Munich, were often managed by old pupils from the Spanish Riding School, the equestrian influence of which predominated the whole of Central Europe.

**Lieutenant Franck
(Swiss Army)**

**Captain Taton
(French Army)
Riding-Master-in-Chief at the Turkish Cavalry School**

THE STAFF OF THE RIDING SCHOOL

The actual staff of the Riding School comprises:

1	Riding Master-in-Chief (*Reitmeister*)
4	First Riding Masters (*Oberbereiter*)
4	Riding Masters (*Bereiter*)
2	Scholars (*Skolar*)
4	Scholar pupils (*Élève*)

The costume worn by the staff is the same today as a hundred years ago, and consists of a black cocked [bi-corn] hat, brown dress-coat buttoned to the neck, high stiff white collar, cream tight-fitting leather breeches, high black leather boots with buckled spurs and a light whip of freshly-cut birch.

It is worth mentioning that several foreign riding masters have, from time to time, been members of the staff of the Riding School. For instance, Count de Montigny was on the staff from 1842 to 1845 after having served several years in a Hungarian regiment of Hussars. He was later Riding Master (*écuyer*) at the Cavalry School at Saumur from 1852 to 1855, and thereafter, Inspector-General of all the training schools (*écoles de dressage*) in France.

EXHIBITION OF RIDING MASTERS

The Salute

Shoulder-in

THE LIPPIZANER

The Lippiza Stud (Karst)

The horses of the Riding School consist exclusively of Lippizan stallions (Lippizaners) of mainly Spanish origin, which, through the centuries, have retained and further developed their aptitude for the special training in High School.

Both the Lippiza Stud and the Riding School were under the direction of the Master of the Horse and the breeding was guided by the results obtained with the stallions in the Riding School.

Until the first World War, the Stud was situated at Lippiza in the Duchy of Carniola (Karst). After World War I, it was moved to Piber in Styria [Austria] and to Hostra in the Sudetes. The Lippizaner — considered pure, althorugh the old Spanish stock has at various times been crossed with Arab, Neapolitan and Danish stock — is represented by five families[4], namely:

---

4   There are two other stallion lines found in eastern Europe. They are accepted as equal to the other six classical lines. They are Tulipan and Incitato, both of Spanish blood, born in 1800 and 1802 respectively.

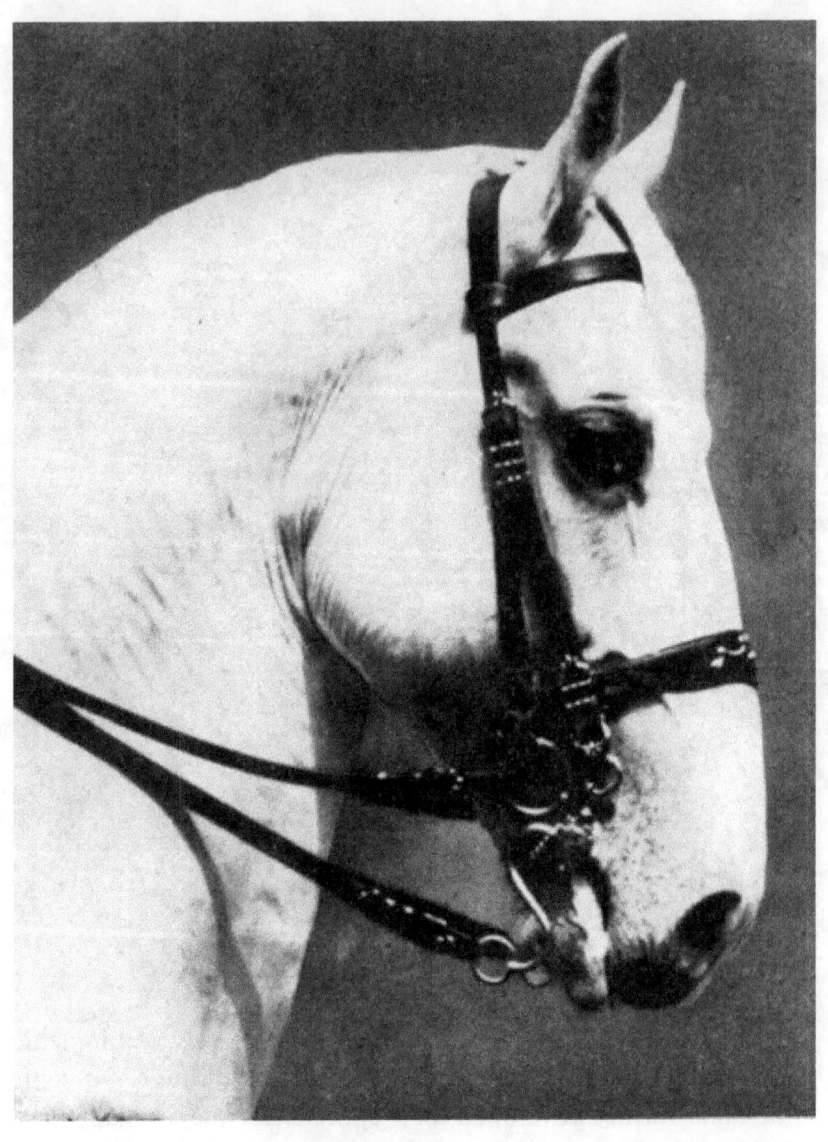

Pluto — white — Danish — born 1765 (Spanish descent)

Conversano — black — Neapolitan — born 1767 (from Naples, Italy)

Neapolitano — bay — Neapolitan — born 1790 (from Polesine, Italy)

Favory — dun — Spanish — born 1779 (at Lippiza)

Maestoso — white — Spanish — born 1773 (in Spain)

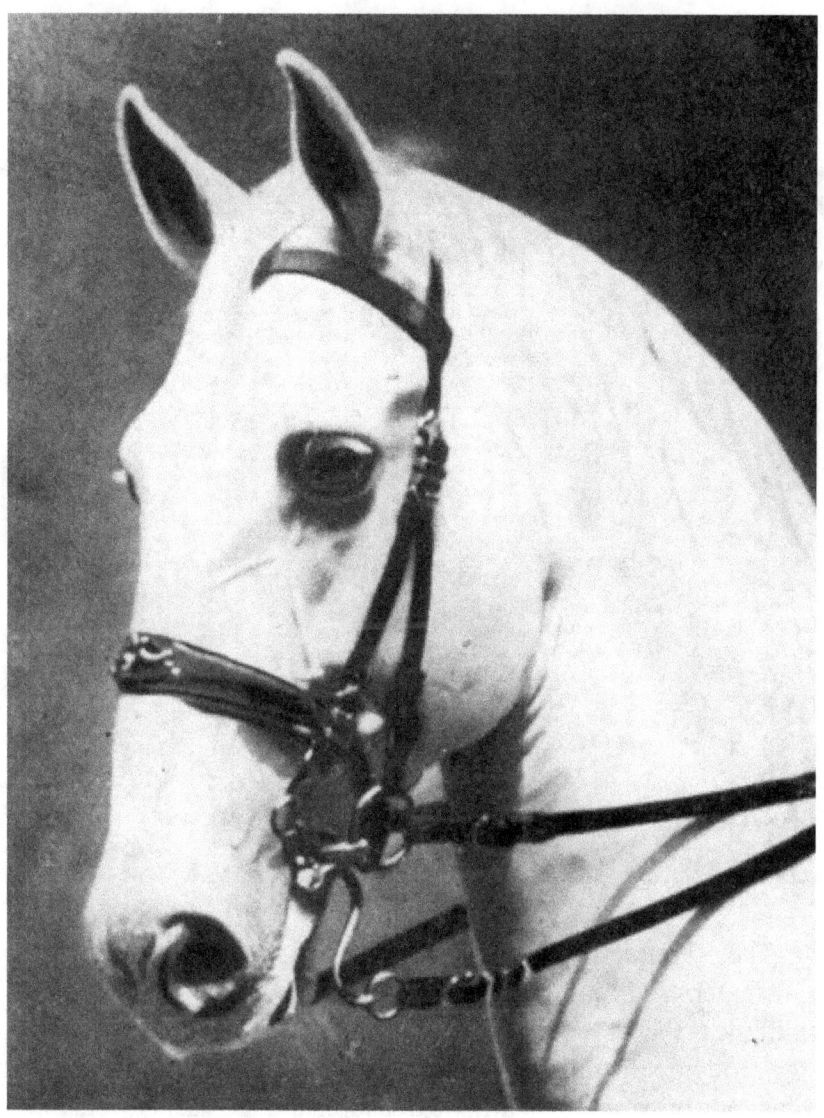

The contribution of Arab blood was made by a stallion from Syria. Further attempts to introduced Arab blood were made between 1840 and 1869 but the Arab line that is retained today descends from:

Siglavy — white — born 1810 (Syria)

The Lippizaner is distinguished by an impressive appearance and noble bearing, although he stands only from fifteen to sixteen hands. Lippizaners have, as a rule, a ram-like nose, large expressive eyes and well-set ears. The withers are low and the back is rather long, but the loins are strong and compact. The croup is muscular and rounded. The legs are extremely strong and the hooves excellent. The most valuable quality of the Lippizaner is, however, his sterling character.

THE RIDING SCHOOL

The Riding School adjoins the Imperial Palace, the Hofburg, in Vienna. Its exterior hardly reveals its purpose, but the impression of its interior is nothing less than over-whelming. The high colonnade which surrounds the *manège* produces a striking perspective effect. It is surmounted by a balcony, the balustrade of which is an artistic treasure, and the vast coffers of the ceiling harmonize admirably with the rest of the interior – all white decorations. The Riding School is practically a replica of Mansard's project for the Chapel of the Château de Versailles (*L'Europe Française,* by V. Réau).

Opposite the main entrance of the *manège* is the Imperial Box displaying the painted portrait of the founder of the Riding School, Emperor Charles VI, life-sized, mounted on a white Lippizaner stallion. Tradition demands that as soon as a rider has mounted a horse he halts on the right rein in front of this portrait and salutes.

At ground-level, below the Imperial Box is a seating area reserved for distinguished visitors, and when a display is staged in honor of such visitors, it is the custom that the Riding Masters in single file canter into this box and trace a circle around them.

**Painting by Julius von Blaas (about 1890).
["Morning Training in the Riding School in the Nineties"]**

A passage under the vault of the old *Burgtor* [castle gate] and crossing the street named Reitschulgasse leads from the Riding School to the Stables. The vaulted ceiling of the stables is corniced in red marble and decorated with sculpted heads of horses. The mangers are also made of red marble and the walls, like those of the Riding School, are snow-white.

There are two reception rooms for visitors, decorated with paintings and engravings showing events and movements from the Riding School and the Lippiza Stud, as well as late Riding Masters. An open-air riding school is situated between the indoor Riding School and the Imperial Palace.

The saddlery is kept in two large saddle-rooms. The regulation bridle is made of black leather with brass buckles and fittings. It has no throat latch and the nose band passes through loops in the cheek pieces which are attached to the curb bit. The saddle is covered with deer-skin and is fitted with a bow roll and a cantle roll. The flaps are practically the same shape as those of the English saddle. A crupper and a big shabrack[5] complete the everyday outfit. For full dress a breastplate is added and the mane is plaited with gold ribbons and three pairs of gold tassels.

---

5 saddlecloth

Reception Room

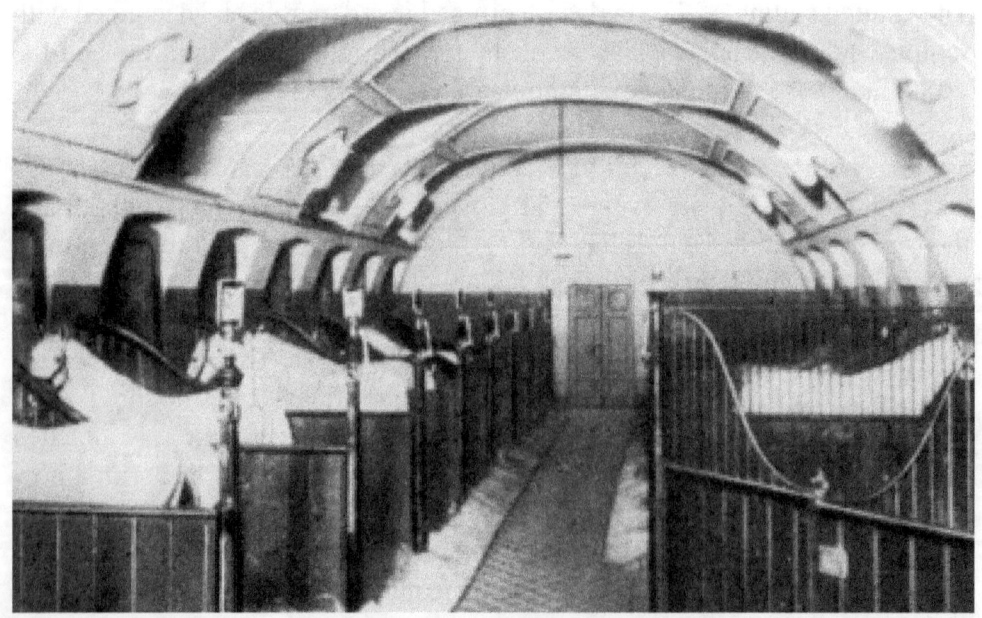
Stables

THE EXHIBITIONS

Painting by L. Koch

Before the last war[6] about twenty full dress exhibitions took place in the Riding School every year. The admission was either free, or for charity. In addition, greatly applauded exhibitions were given from time to time at major horse shows in foreign cities; for example, in London, Brussels, The Hague and Hilversum.

These exhibitions were arranged in order to give the public a clear picture of the progress of schooling the stallions from the beginning to the end of training, from the young stallion just arrived at the Riding School to the finished High School horse, showing the work in-hand, between the pillars and on the long-rein, as well as mounted.

The program included all the gaits and airs of the *Haute École*, the Quadrille, the *Pas-de-deux* and the Reprise of twelve Riding Masters [quadrille].

---

6 World War II

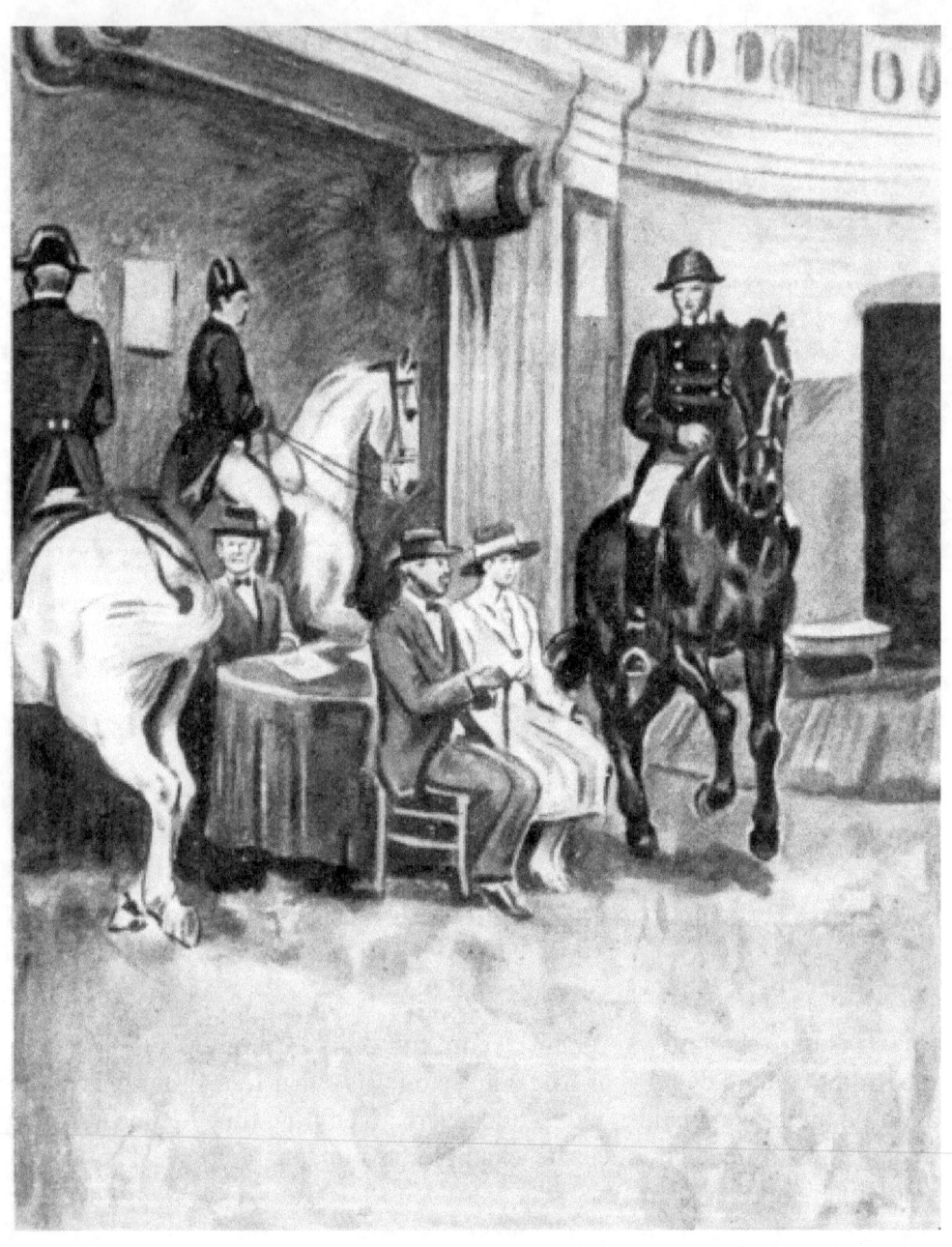

Painting by L. Koch

No exhibitions take place during the summer months which are usually very hot, and the stallions are rested at the Zoological Gardens at Linz [Austria].

THE PRINCIPLES OF THE METHOD OF TRAINING

François Robichon de la Guérinière
SHOULDER-IN

The Vienna School proclaims its unshaken fidelity towards the principles of Robichon de la Guérinière [*École de Cavalerie,* Xenophon Press 1992, 2013] and considers its own famous Riding Masters to be the direct heirs of this old Master.

These principles of training are passed on by word of mouth, very few written documents being in existence. The Riding Master-in-Chief, Niedermayer (1865-87), left some notes which, unfortunately, have not been published. Some directions for the methodical training were given by F. M. L. von Hohlwein, First Equerry, towards the end of the nineteenth century as follows:

The art of riding and training the horse does not consider the *Haute École* in isolation. On the contrary, it embraces the following three stages:

1. Work on the straight line at the natural gaits and position of the horse.
2. Outdoor riding, gradually obtaining balance of the horse through collection and suppling exercises.
3. Work in artificial balance created by complete flexion and lowering of the haunches, in all of the natural gaits out of which are derived all of the airs of the *Haute École*,

This order of the three stages must be adhered to. Only the first stage might be considered independent of the other two. The second cannot be obtained without the first, and third stage should only follow from the first and second stages.

The characteristics of the *Haute École* should be the highest possible degree of suppleness and is only legitimate to the degree that it actually increases the qualities of the horse in its usefulness for outdoor riding.

Colonel von Oeynhausen

THE METHOD OF TRAINING

Débourrage [Beginning of Training]

The Lippizaner develops rather late. The young stallions arrive at the Riding School in the autumn as four-year-olds.

The breaking-in is carried out very slowly and cautiously and usually lasts two years.

The first work consists of lunging the horse with side reins which are adjusted in such a way that light contact with the horse's mouth is maintained without constraining his neck.

When the horse is sufficiently strong and developed, one gives the lesson of mounting on the lunge. Then he is ridden during a part of the lunge lesson, which is accordingly extended for a longer period. The rider, for the sake of habituating the horse to his weight, remains absolutely passive in the saddle until complete confidence is obtained mainly through talking to and caressing the horse. Then he takes up the snaffle reins, the aid of which gradually replaces the aid of the lunge line. As soon as an equal and light feel of both snaffle reins is established, the horse is ridden at slow gaits after the removal of the lunging line and the side reins.

The lessons should never be long enough to tire the horse.

In the beginning the horse is permitted to stretch and lower his head and neck in order not to interfere with the action of the back muscles. All that is desired is a good contact with the horse's mouth without raising his head.

The horse is thus ridden at the three gaits: walk, trot and canter, the latter being obtained from a trot or a walk passing a corner of the school. These are well rounded during the breaking-in period as the aim is to ride the horse straight forward as far as possible. Consequently, no circles or turns, or by implication obedience to the aid of any one of the rider's legs, are asked.

Toward the end of the second year, the rider begins to regulate the various gaits without raising the horse's neck.

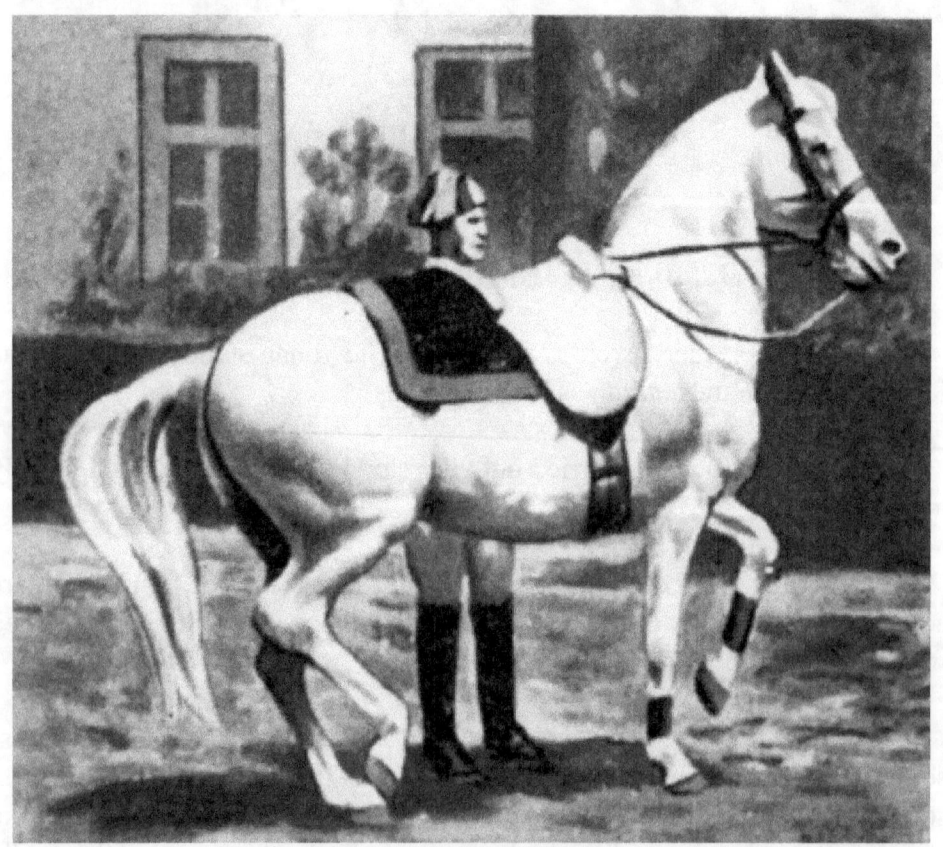

Work on the hand—Piaffe

Work on the hand—Levade

Work on the hand—Levade

Work on the hand—Levade

DRESSAGE

The dressage is not started until the forces [strength] of the horse permit it.

The raising of the horse's neck should be the result of the gradual lowering of the quarters in connection with increased impulsion from the hind legs and should not be obtained by means of the reins. The same applies to the direct flexion at the poll and vertical position of the head.

The impulsion is maintained by the aids of the legs and the whip. The spurs are used very sparingly and only at a rather advanced stage of the training; in fact, often not until the teaching of the airs of the *Haute École*.

Running reins are used occasionally, but only in order to maintain the normal position of the horse's head and not to obtain the direct flexion at the poll. Or, following the words of the Riding Masters, they constitute a defensive and not an offensive aid.

The horse is slightly bent to the curve of the circle described when changing directions and in the lateral movements. In the latter, it is prescribed that the rider's shoulders and hips should be parallel to the horse's shoulders and hips respectively.

The lateral movements are only practiced for short spells at a time and usually at an angle not exceeding 40 degrees [to the track].

At the end of the Dressage period, the movement at the walk, trot and canter should be more elevated, condensed and collected than at the corresponding natural gaits.

The high degree of collection required for the gaits and airs of the *Haute École* at the Vienna School is usually obtained, or at least prepared, through the work "on the hand[7]" and in the pillars. However, the latter is not considered indispensable and horses that are too timid or violent (extremely rare) are not trained in the pillars at all.

---

7   in the hand

Hand Work

This work is started once the horse has learned to go well into his bridle on the lunge line, pushes well from behind, and easily keeps his head in the vertical position [*ramener*] by adjusting the side reins.

The horse is then placed along the wall, the Riding Master standing at his inside shoulder and holding the shortened lunge line [short line] and a whip. The horse is asked to collect progressively at the walk by touching the horse with the whip at the base of the haunches until he is able to easily maintain a slow, cadenced trot. Little by little, the trot is shortened until he can do it in one place [the piaffe.] When begun from the halt, the piaffe is not asked to be strictly on the spot [it should advance.]

Piaffe

Capriole

Courbette

Capriole

Work on the Long Reins

The Riding Masters in Vienna also work their horses on the long reins. The reins, however, do not pass through any rings on the girth, but go directly from the bit to the Riding Master's hand like a pair of long riding reins. The stallions are so gentle that the Riding Master can follow at arm's length either by the side of the horses or directly behind the croup, in order to be able to easily touch the horse wid the hand.

Levade

Passage

Work on the Long Reins

Capriole in the pillars, to which the horse is not attached

Passage

Work in the Pillars

No horse is trained in the pillars without fulfilling the following two conditions:

1. Having been completely trained in the elementary school, including the lateral movements at the school walk, trot, and canter.
2. Having learned to perform the piaffe calmly with regularity "on the hand."

Side reins and long reins (no doubt to make it easier to keep the horse straight) are sometimes used while training the horse in the pillars. The piaffe is taught, first without and then with a rider, who remains completely passive. Gradually the hindquarters should be lowered and the cadence becomes slower. Under no circumstances is it permitted to touch the horse's forelegs with the whip. Their elevated action should be the result of the activity of the hind.

Levade between the Pillars

legs.

Work in the Pillars

Levade in the Pillars

THE HAUTE ÉCOLE

Mounted work

When the horse has learned the piaffe in the pillars with a passive rider in the saddle, it is time to teach him the same outside the pillars. The Riding Master on foot applies the aids, in place of which the aids of the rider are gradually substituted.

When the horse understands the aids of the rider, he is made to move slowly forward at the piaffe thus gradually developing the passage.

Most horses in the school are trained to passage in this way. However, there are some horses with a marked talent for this movement that are taught

PIAFFER
Riding-Master-in-Chief Polak

the passage from the school trot. In these cases, the piaffe is obtained by shortening the passage.

The piaffe is the one air of the *Haute École* which, more than any other, characterizes the style of this Riding School. It is always performed with perfect regularity, is often brilliant and, as far as the best disposed stallions are concerned, is remarkably majestic.

The regularity is due to the excellent balance of the stallions. Without being overloaded, the hindquarters are lowered just sufficiently to permit the joints to support the excess weight and make the hind legs move with undiminished energy and correctness.

Owing to the thick neck of the stallions it is not always possible to obtain the correct vertical position of the head, but when this is possible the piaffe of the Lippizaner is performed with a cadence of majestic slowness due

PIAFFE
Riding-Master-in-Chief Polak

PIAFFE
Riding-Master-in-Chief Lindenbauer

to the long duration of the moment of suspension when changing from the one diagonal to the other.

The neck is, as a result of the training and without using force, sufficiently raised to lighten the shoulders and cause the brilliant action of the forelegs.

PIAFFE
Chief Rider Meixner

**PIAFFE
Riding-Master-
in-Chief
Lindenbauer**

PIAFFE

The Passage shows the same graceful ease and powerful elasticity as the Piaffe, whether developed from or perfected by this movement.[8]

The change from the one movement to the other takes place without the slightest disturbance of the beats which are lengthened or shortened without losing their regularity and strict cadence.

Artificial fancy movements such as the Spanish Walk and the Spanish Trot which have no place in the classical *Haute École* are not practiced at the Vienna School.

Passage

---

8   piaffe

Passage

PASSAGE
Chief Rider Lindenbauer

THE SCHOOL CANTER

The exercises at the canter comprise, in addition to the School Canter, the Redopp, the Mezair and the Pirouette. The Redopp is a lateral movement more elevated than the School Canter and from which the Pirouette is developed. The Mezair is still more elevated and serves as a preparatory exercise for the School Springs [jumps]. The Pirouette is performed at the cadence of the School Canter but with greater elevation of the forehand. The changing of the leading legs is not carried further than to changing every second stride [at the time of original publication, 1947].

School Canter

Canter Pirouette to the Left

THE SCHOOL JUMPS [AIRS]

The school jumps practiced in Vienna [airs] include the Levade, the Courbette, the Croupade, the Ballotade, and the Capriole [and formerly the Mezair.]

Their definitions, according to the principles of the Vienna School, are included in the Program at the end of the next section and are identical with those given in 1778 by Montfaucon de Rogles, the only Riding Master of the Versailles School who left a written account on the teaching of this school [at the time of original publication, 1947].

Mezair

The following points should be noted:

1. The movement called "Levade" at the Vienna School was termed "Pesade" at the School of Versailles. In both cases the horse raises his forehand and keeps his hind legs firmly and motionlessly on the ground, all the joints of the hindquarters being bent as much as possible.

2. That the air which today is termed "Courbette" in France is nothing but a "High Pesade." At the Versailles School this air was obtained by making the horse perform the ordinary [low] Pesade and then extend his strongly bent hocks (*préalablement fléchis*) [previously flexed then opening to a higher angle], whereas at the Saumur School the "courbette" is obtained directly [with more open hocks and omitting the preceding deep pesade done at the Spanish Riding School, prior to the courbette.]

Levade

High Levade (Pesade)

Levade

3   This Courbette or "High Pesade" is quite different from the classical Courbette which, according to Montfaucon, is a spring forward in the position of the Pesade.

4   The movement which in France today is called "Croupade" and consists only of the horse standing still with his front leges and kicking with his hind legs, is not classical. Consequently, it is not included in the airs of the Versailles and Vienna schools.

5   The classical Croupade practiced in the Versailles and Vienna schools has nothing in common with the previously explained air. It is, according to Montfaucon, a jump with the hind legs being tucked up close to the belly.

6   As far as the Capriole is concerned, the aim of the Vienna School is to make the horse kick with his hind legs horizontally the moment the forehand is in its highest position, in order to enable the horse to land with all four legs simultaneously[9]. In France, however, the aim is to make the horse kick with his hind legs as high as possible above the horizontal, and at a later stage of the jump. The movement is thus like that of a natural jump over a fence, the horse landing with his forelegs first.

---

9   This landing with all four legs simultaneously has never been recorded photographically [1947] and must be considered a rather unnatural ideal which is very seldom attained in practice.

Mezair

Levade

Courbette

Capriole

Courbette

The Phases of the CAPRIOLE

Caprioles

LINDENBAUER:
RIDING MASTER-IN-CHIEF

Lindenbauer, the present [1947] Riding Master-in-Chief, has, in addition to all the eminent qualities of his predecessors, one quality which places him in the ranks of the most illustrious.

In addition to the rigorous precision of the application of the aids and the elegant and correct seat which has always been a characteristic of the Riding Masters of the School, he has a most delicate hand, a point which not long ago left something to be desired in several of his predecessors.

His horses, like those of Weyrother and Oeynhausen, perform all their work on a very light rein and with the perfect "lightness," which is the touchstone of the true *Haute École*. There is no doubt that the School under his leadership will regain the fame of the most illustrious periods in its history. But the necessary means for maintaining it must be found with the aid of the Allies. That is the wish of all those who are anxious to preserve this artistic legacy, the joint property of all nations.

Maximilian von Weyrother

Colonel C.T. von Oeynhausen

PROGRAM OF A GALA EXHIBITION 1934

EXHIBITION
at the "Spanish Riding School," Hofburg, Vienna
accompanied by the Dengler-Nowak sextette
(French horn quintette and trumpet)
members of the National Opera and of the Robert Dreschler Band.

PROGRAM
1.
Introduction-Fanfare .... by J. Schantl
Polonaise .... by F. Chopin

Young Stallions:
Pluto Austria .... First Riding Master Lindenbauer
Conversano Capriola .... First Riding Master Polak
Favory Pluto II .... Riding Master Resch
Pluto Austria II .... Riding Master Lippert

2.

Toskana, Fanfare ....…..……. by J. Schantl
Die Schoenbrunner, Waltz …………….............……………... by J. Lanner

Hand and Pillar Work:

Conversano Presciana ………...…………. First Riding Master Lindenbauer
Pluto Siglavy ………………………........………… First Riding Master Polak
Neapolitano Betalka ………………........………….. Riding Master Neumayer
Pluto Kerka ……………………….........…………….… Riding Master Cerha
Conversano Stornella …………………........………….. Riding Master Resch

3.

Jagdlust, Fanfare ……………………………..................……. by K. Stiegler
a) Die Lautenschlaegerin, Gavotte …....……………….. by K. Komzak
b) Natalie, Gavotte ………………………........…………. by G. Richter

All the Movements and Airs of the *Haute École*:

Conversano Presciana …………………… First Riding Master Lindenbauer
Favory Montenegra ……….........…………….. First Riding Master Polak
Neapolitano Betalka ………………........………….. Riding Master Neumayer
Conversano Alba ….............………………………….… Riding Master Cerha
Conversano Nobila ……………….........…………….. Riding Master Resch
Favory Pluto I …..........……………………………….. Riding Master Lippert

4.

Schloss Frankenstein, Fanfare ……………………............…….. by F. Dengler
Holzschuh, Polka …………...…………….......………… by C. W. Drescher

Pas de Deux:

Conversano Bonavista …...……………….. First Riding Master Lindenbauer
Conversano Nobila ………………..…….........……... Riding Master Resch

5.

Luetzows wilde Jagd, Fanfare ……..........…..……………………. by J. Schantl
A jour, Quick-Polka ……………………..…………….. by C. W. Drescher

Test of Obedience:

Conversano Alba ………………….................................. Riding Master Cerha
Conversano Nobila …………..........………………….… Riding Master Resch
Maestoso Sardinia ……………………..……..………... Riding Master Lippert

6.

Heroldfanfare .... by A. Stark
Vienna Waltz Potpourri .... by R. Drescher

School Springs:

Neapolitano Adriana (Levade) .... Riding Master Cerha
Favory Bionda (Mezair) .... First Riding Master Lindenbauer
Conversano Stornella (Levade) .... Riding Master Resch
Maestoso Theodorosta (Courbette) .... Riding Master Lippert
Neapolitano Sardinia (Capriole) .... First Riding Master Polak

7.

Jaegers Wanderliedchen .... by A. Wunderer
a)   Stefanie, Gavotte .... by A. Cibulka
b)   Mondschein, Gavotte .... by Z. Gruenecke

On the Long Reins:

Neapolitano Bionda .... First Riding Master Polak

8.

Meran, Fanfare .... by J. Schantl
Quadrille Excelsior .... by J. Marenko

Quadrille:

Conversano Presciana .... First Riding Master Lindenbauer
Conversano Alba .... Riding Master Cerha
Neapolitano Afrika .... Riding Master Resch
Neapolitano Montenuova .... Riding Master Lippert

The preceeding program is subject to change as needed.
Entrance fee: 50 Silbergros (500 pfennigs)

EXPLANATION OF THE PROGRAM

I. Young Stallions.
The young horses, exclusively stallions, are four-year-olds, sent from the State Stud, "Piber" in Styria to the Spanish School in Vienna, where they are worked on the lunging rein for about three months and then gradually and cautiously ridden. The Lippizaners require a longer time to develop than other horses, and consequently, last longer and reach a greater age.

II. Hand and Pillar Work.
In the second year a more intensive training is started commencing with the piaffe in hand[10]. If a horse is gifted, he is put to work in the pillars. This generally discloses the horse's aptitude for the airs of the *Haute École* (Passage, Levade, Courbette, Capriole etc.) for which the particular horse is most adapted. Only the talents naturally possessed by a horse are developed and continuously perfected in accordance with the principles of the *Haute École* originating from the 16th century. Artificial movements, which belong to the circus and not to the classical art of equitation, are strictly excluded. During the third year the work is continued progressively. The single snaffle which has been used up till now is replaced by the double bridle.

III. All the Movements and Airs of the *Haute École*.
These are performed by the completely schooled horses.

IV. Pas de Deux.
An exhibition of [two] particularly well-schooled [*bien 'mis'*] horses [under saddle]. The ability to rigorously maintain the correct rhythm and exact tracking is especially important in this mirror image presentation of voltes, serpentines and other movements.

V. Test of Obedience.
Demonstration of the high degree of obedience and ability of the horses.

VI. School Springs.
These include the traditional airs of the *Haute École* in which the horse either raises his forehand off the ground or performs a spring, namely the Levade, Mezair, Courbette, Croupade, Ballotade and Capriole.

---

10   *à la main, (cheval non monté)*[literally: "to the hand" (horse not mounted); currently this is called 'in-hand work" or "hand work" or "on the hand"]

The Levade: A stationary air in which the horse raises his forehand with the forelegs drawn up in a bent position resting on his hind legs with all the joints of the hindquarters bent as much as possible.

The Mezair: A Levade, the horse advancing. Starting from the Levade, the horse puts both forelegs to the ground simultaneously and advances a short step with both hind legs simultaneously, immediately raising his forehand again in the Levade, and so on several times in succession.

The Courbette: A series of springs forward on the hind legs, the forehand remaining in the position of the Levade and the forelegs consequently not touching the ground.

The Croupade: A single spring into the air without gaining ground, the hind legs being drawn up close to the belly.

The Ballotade: A single spring like the Croupade, but with the hind legs in such a position that the shoes can be seen from behind the horse as if the horse was about to kick.

The Capriole: The most perfect and difficult School Spring. It is a single spring into the air in which the horse kicks out violently with both hind legs.

VII. On the Long Reins.

Demonstration of a perfectly trained horse peforming on the long reins all the movements and airs of the *Haute École*, the Riding Master applying the aids of the reins and the whip only, the latter aid being very light.

VIII. Quadrille.

The quadrille must be performed with particular accuracy in order to produce a pleasing effect and, therefore, requires the most perfectly trained horses.

Following principles which date back several centuries, the Spanish Riding School strictly adheres to the ancient and traditional customs. Still, the purpose of the School today is essentially practical, namely to train experienced riders and, at the same time, school selected stallions, the best of which are eventually returned for breeding purposes to the Piber stud, the present-day home of the Lippizaner. Consequently, the Spanish Riding School is the place where the Lippizaners are tested and selected for their capacities.

PIAFFE AND PASSAGE

Preparation for Dressage Tests

by General Decarpentry

With a Preface
by Colonel Danloux

Translated to English
by Patricia Galvin

Edited by Richard F. Williams

© Xenophon Press 2013

Piaffe and Passage

by General Decarpentry

Translated by Patricia Galvin

"Professeur"

Thoroughbred by *Jacobi* out of *Sainte-Enimie*
September 1931

XENOPHON PRESS

PREFACE TO "PIAFFE AND PASSAGE" XENOPHON PRESS EDITION

Pierre Danloux begins his preface of Decarpentry's book, small by its size but big by its importance, by telling us that the riders of his time were not very good at piaffe and passage. Today, not much has changed. Piaffe and passage remain the central training issues that frustrate many riders. A progression that uses a huge trot full of energy and calls it "collected" doesn't lead very easily to trotting in place in relaxation. An equitation based on forceful aids doesn't foster the delicacy needed to organize the self-carriage indispensable to piaffe, passage, and the transitions between them.

There is more than one way to teach these movements and there are many more solutions to correct the problems that unavoidably occur in their training. Based on the work he did with his Thoroughbred horse, *Professeur*, Decarpentry gives us practical solutions to the problems he encountered with this particular horse, possibly not universal problems to all the horses we may encounter in our career. Training a Thoroughbred to piaffe presents its own set of challenges: they need a longer, more careful and systematic preparation due to their excitable temperaments. Decarpentry's techniques apply well to today's Trakehners and hotter warmbloods of the modern type and may be different from training older type warmbloods that need a little infusion of excitement to perform.

Both the piaffe and passage obtained from *Professeur*, a slightly downhill built Thoroughbred, a breed not necessarily the easiest to train to the epitome of high school, gives high credit to Decarpentry's ability as a true "*écuyer-professeur*" capable of training, explaining and writing with mastery about his subject. The exclusive use of the curb throughout the work is different from modern practice and this book doesn't give any hint on the work-in-hand preparation Decarpentry may have used with his horse (a technique of which he was a reputed master). Still, this seminal book provides us with a window of "reality training," a true "journal of dressage" in which the trainer hides nothing and tells us of his difficulties as well as his eventual success. He talks to us with honesty and modesty, not pretending that this is the only valid method to train a horse in these difficult movements, but that this is the one he used for this particular horse, and suggests techniques well worth trying.

The 1932 Olympic Champion, Xavier Lesage, Decarpentry's friend and student, said of him (in a letter to Colonel Challan Belval after Decarpentry's death):

"He was a very good rider, much slower than General Wattel[1], only passing from one stage to the next after eliminating every resistance he encountered. He always advised never to leave unattended resistances because one might always find them again at the most inopportune moment. He had less power in his legs than Wattel, because of his handicap due to a wound received during the 1914-1918 War....

"Very methodical, he worked very quietly, without fanfare or showing off to the gallery; I have never seen him in an open fight with his horse. He sat well on a horse, had much discretion in his aids and we could tell he was very observant and focused on finding the slightest resistance.

"He was also a master in the art of work-in-hand that he practiced very wisely, sending his horse on a hand that only presented the right amount of opposition, avoiding, at all costs, excessive rounding of the loins. Instead, he sought a supple engagement of the hind legs coming under the centre.

"How much I have regretted being unable to work with him regularly and benefit from his teaching.

"However, he had unlimited time and he would make sure to never forget a resistance, as it has happened to us many times as we were pressed for time in the preparation of a show on a fixed date, as you well know. Colonel Danloux ribbed him a little bit about the time he took to polish the training of his horses. He had a tendency to split hairs in the dressage of his horses, as is apparent in his books, but once again, he had time."

The current sketchy quality of many public performances of piaffe and passage warrants serious study of the solutions already discovered by the past masters. Decarpentry demonstrates the training of a Thoroughbred and not the training of Iberian horses, explained by the masters of the baroque and classical era of the School of Versailles. The baroque breeds present a different set of problems from modern sport horses and respond well to the use of the pillars, a method rarely used today. The technique discussed by Decarpentry (the development of collection through repeated halts from trot and departs back to trot) is a skill that all dressage horses need to acquire. The transition to the passage from piaffe and from the trot to the passage are described in great detail. Real lightness to hand and leg aids is key to achieving brilliance in genuinely happy horses "enjoying themselves in their airs," and is the true essence of Equestrian Art, a fact that is all too often forgotten. This excellent book by Decarpentry is the perfect place to begin the study of piaffe and passage, and to learn about important training advice needed to correct problems.

-Jean Philippe Giacomini
Lexington, Kentucky, June 2013

---

[1] famous Chief Rider of Saumur and a famous dressage virtuoso of that period

NOTE ON THE TRANSLATION
BY PATRICIA GALVIN

Many equestrian terms are as elusive [in their meanings] as their definitions. For the purposes of this text, new terms have been adopted for those which have no precise English translation. I would like to specify two of special importance, with their more classical French definitions:

BALANCE IN HAND (*mise en main*) means a light and supple connection with the mouth of the horse in complete submission to the hand of the rider. There must be neither resistance of the horse's weight (a passive resistance resulting from a faulty equilibrium, with too much weight on the forehand), nor of the horse's force (an active resistance of the muscles in the neck and jaw). The horse may be *balanced in hand* by keeping the natural carriage of his head and neck, as long as he has this light and willing communication with the rider's hand.

THE *RAMENER*[2] concerns the position of the forehand. The horse must have a supple and elevated neck, flexion at the poll, and a loose and relaxed jaw. These conditions result in an approximately vertical position of the head.

When the horse is *ramener*[3], he is also balanced in hand, but he may be balanced in hand without being in the *ramener*.

-*Patricia Galvin*

[NOTE: About Patricia Galvin, translator.

We owe the original translation of this work to Patricia Galvin (later the Princess of La Tour d'Auvergne after her French marriage). This American rider rode the Irish bred Thoroughbred gelding, Rath Patrick, at Aachen and in two Pan American Games, where he won each time. She also participated in two Olympic Games (1960 Rome Games where she was 6th and 1964 Tokyo Games where she led the U.S. Team to a 4th place thanks to her 8th individual placing). Galvin and Rath Patrick owed a special debt to Decarpentry. General Durand,

2   [Originally P. Galvin used the term "The Gathering (*ramener*)" here. "Gathering" is a loose definition of the French word *rassembler* and not a definition of *ramener*. Here we correct the definition of *ramener* and later will quote Decarpentry himself for the correct definition of *rassembler*.]

3   [Originally P. Galvin used the term "*gathered*" here, but Decarpentry uses the word *ramener*, the rounding of the neck to bring the horse's forehead to the vertical position.]

former Chief Rider and Director of Saumur, reminds us in his preface to *"The Advice of General Decarpentry to a Young Rider"* (Favre Ed.):

"The Canadian, Leonard R. Lafond trained the horse, Rath Patrick by following to the letter the teaching of Decarpentry and completed it by a course at Saumur before the Stockholm Games where he finished in front of the French competitors."

After the death of Lafond, Patricia Galvin acquired Rath Patrick and went on to the successes we know.

She was coached for years by the Olympic rider and author Jean Saint-Fort Paillard and Jean Salmon. She visited Oliveira in Lisbon with Saint-Fort Paillard where she was quite taken by Oliveira's talent and the beauty of his horses' piaffe and passage, according to Captain de Fombelle, another show jumper, who was present.

Patricia Galvin de la Tour d'Auvergne was a passionate observer of dressage masters. She tells us in *"Dressage for Girls and Grandmothers,"* edited by William Steinkraus:

"I have watched the dressage masters and they all seem to have a sort of Buddhistic detachment, an intense concentration on things like walking on a straight line, endlessly playing with a horse's mouth until he gives just as he should, or monotonously starting and stopping at X until the watcher is bored to death. Dressage's magic formula is the overpowering force of gentleness and repetition."

This seems to adroitly describe Decarpentry's painstaking approach to his preparation for piaffe and passage.

I also point out the importance of the Galvin family as sponsors of equestrian sports on two continents. William Steinkraus, the Olympic gold medallist, wrote:

"The U.S.E.T. and I personally, will be eternally grateful to Sir John Galvin's family and especially to Trish, the Princess de la Tour d'Auvergne, the wonderful dressage rider, for their generosity in making available to the show jumping team such horses as Snowbound, San Lucas and Night Owl." (all international and Olympic competitors for the U.S.A.).

John Galvin also set up a stable in Maisons-Lafitte near Paris for international French dressage riders to train in an adequate facility. It is in this spirit of sponsorship and promotion that Patricia Galvin has made this work of Decarpentry available to English speaking readers.

-Jean Philippe Giacomini

PREFACE
BY COLONEL PIERRE DANLOUX

Écuyer en chef à l'École de Saumur (Chief Rider of the Cadre Noir, Saumur)

Piaffer and Passage comes at the right time [1931] and answers a precise purpose: to facilitate the task of riders preparing for the difficult Olympic test[4].

Working alone as they usually do, they only achieve mediocre results in these two movements. They lack a guide to lead them on the road of progress.

They will certainly find the best of counsel in these few pages, dictated by experience and written so temperately and clearly, in which the author, with a sincerity and modesty that do him credit, does not hesitate to criticize his own performance in order to make himself better understood.

You, my dear Decarpentry, are especially qualified to treat this difficult subject.

When you and I were *sous-écuyers*[5] together, and most of us were doing more d'Aure[6] than Baucher[7], were you not already trying to pierce the

4   [That was to come in 1932 in Los Angeles, CA, USA, where Colonel Lesage, another Cadre Noir equerry and future head rider, eventually won the individual Gold medal with the Thoroughbred, Taine, as well as the team Gold with Marion and Jousseaume.]

5   ["under-equerries", below the level of master riders or "equerries"]

6   Count Antoine Cartier d'Aure (1799–1863) was a riding master in France. He was the arch rival of François Baucher, and their repective methods differed greatly. He was born in Toulouse, southwest France. He graduated from the Military Academy, St Cyr in 1817 and later joined the "Grand Stable" ("*Grande Ecurie*") of the Palace of Versailles as an assistant instructor under the direction of Viscount Pierre-Marie d'Abzac, the most famous equerry of his time in the whole of Europe. He later directed the "Grand Stable" and was its last Chief Rider for Kings Louis XVIII and Charles X. D'Aure was the chief trainer of the Riding School in Saumur (1847–1854), where he was accepted over François Baucher. While there, he promoted steeplechasing, hunting and the use of extended walk and trot to help with the training of the horses. D'Aure was a strong opponent of the methods of Baucher. D'Aure was appointed the Director of the stables of Napoléon III and then named as General Inspector of the National Stud Farms in 1861.

7   François Baucher (1796–1873) was a French riding master whose methods are still hotly debated by dressage enthusiasts as they diverge from those of many earlier masters. In spite of all the controversy, Baucher still has a strong following today. He took great pride in his ability to produce a horse quickly, claiming to have trained horses to perform the airs within a few months. He is reputed to have invented the one tempi changes, a movement that was considered impossible before

mysteries of the *rassembler*[8]? And at Saumur twenty years later, in your brilliant and precise work with your horse Professeur, have I not found you forever aiming, above all, at perfect lightness?

Now, sending me the proofs of your treatise, you have been kind enough to ask me for a preface; may these lines from your old friend serve the purpose, plain though they may be.

    -P. DANLOUX[9]   Saumur, France, this 15th of August 1932

---

him. Baucher published a number of works on equitation, including the *Dictionnaire raisonné d'équitation*, "Reasoned dictionary of equitation" in 1833; the *Dialogues sur l'équitation*, "Dialogues on equitation" (with Louis Charles Pellier) in 1835 now included in *Francois Baucher: The Man and His Method* by Hilda Nelson, Xenophon Press, 2013; and the *Passe-temps équestres*, "Equestrian pastimes" in 1840.

Baucher's most celebrated work is the *Méthode d'équitation basée sur de nouveaux principes*, "Method of riding based on new principles"; the earliest extant edition is the third, published in 1842. The numerous following editions up to 1863, when his contract with his publishers expired, are essentially reprints of the same book. The 12th edition, published in 1864 and called the *deuxième manière* or second manner, contained notable changes from his original method, and was continued in his 13th edition published in 1868. Captain Raabe was the greatest exponent of the First Manner, while General Faverot de Kerbrech represented the Second manner in his book, *The Methodical Dressage of the Riding Horse...*, Xenophon Press, 2010.

8   "The *Rassembler* (collection) is the disposition of the horse's body which affects all of its parts and places each one in the best position to ensure the most efficient use of the energy produced by the efforts of the hind legs.

"Those efforts can have an immediate and special purpose, or can be a preparation for several eventual purposes....In the first place, it [the collection] must ensure to the horse the maximum mobility in all directions and the ability to make rapid changes of speed. Furthermore, it must enable him, in answer to his rider's command, instantly to impart to his gaits the maximum elevation compatible with the length of stride that the rider wishes to maintain.

"On the one hand, mobility requires a short base of support and this is possible only if the hind legs touch the ground further forward than they would at a free pace, i.e. that they engage [under the body].

"On the other hand, it requires that the mass be held constantly in a mean position so that the center of gravity of the body will remain as close as possible to the vertical line passing through the center of each of the successive bases."
-*Academic Equitation*, General Decarpentry, Nicole Bartel translator, J.A.Allen, 1987
9   Pierre Danloux, (1878-1943) Chief rider of The Cadre Noir (1929-1933), trained by Commander Montjou, who was trained by General L'Hotte. With the Italian Alvisi, Danloux advocated the forward balanced seat method of Federico Caprilli. He shortened the stirrups for jumping, redesigned the jumping saddle, with larger knee rolls to support this new method: alleviating pressure from the horse's back and improving the rider's ability to absorb impact upon landing and horse and rider's balance for jumping.

INTRODUCTION

Foreign critics agree in acknowledging the high quality of the work at the canter presented by nearly all the French contestants in international dressage tests.

They are also unanimous in qualifying the piaffe and the passage of the same competitors, except for a few very brilliant exceptions, in less flattering terms.

Our piaffe is often scored as "sketchy," "indicated," "satisfactory," or "even"; its high and ample style (in a word, its stateliness) never rouses the enthusiasm of the critics who are often unstinted in praise of our single tempi changes, for example.

But this is not surprising, since the courses at Saumur for *sous-lieutenants* and *lieutenants* go as far as the flying changes of lead at the canter but exclude instruction in piaffe and passage.

Most of our [French] competitors have taken only these two courses and consequently are less prepared to complete the training of their horses at the trot than at the canter.[10]

It has seemed to me that it would be useful for them to have a program based on the precepts of our great masters in equitation. I have appended a few observations on putting these precepts into practice in the form of critical notes accompanying photographs of a certain horse and a certain rider with whose shortcomings I am only too well-acquainted.[11]

---

10   The complete course, which includes teaching the whole of classical equitation, has only recently been instituted, and is taken by a very small number of officers. (1932)

11   All the photographs of Colonel Decarpentry and his horse *Professeur*, taken at the École de Cavalerie in Saumur, are by Blanchaud.

Part 1:
Piaffe and Passage

THE SUITABLE ORDER
IN WHICH TO STUDY THESE TWO AIRS

The rule laid down by the old school, and by that of Baucher, was to undertake first the piaffe, and then, with forward impulsion, the passage.

On the other hand, Fillis and Saint-Phalle first undertook the passage, which they then slowed down to achieve the piaffe.

Beyond question, these movements can be brought to perfection by either method when they are taught to the horse by a master.

For horsemen of less skill, however, and in view of the present dressage tests of the Federation Équestre Internationale [F.E.I.], the practice of the old school is to be preferred for the following reasons:

1. The style of the passage as developed from the piaffe is in general more academic and conforms more closely to the definition of the *Federation Équestre Internationale* ["Grand Passage"] in the lifting of the forearms, the bending of the knees, the vertical position of the cannons, and the raising of the fore and hind legs in relation to each other, whereas the passage developed from the trot is more extended than elevated and is less classic in style[12].

2. Certain irregularities of diagonal gaits, often nearly imperceptible at the trot, are still difficult to discern in the passage even though they always become worse in that movement and appear most clearly in the piaffe.

When the piaffe is developed from the passage, and consequently is a result of long-continued work during which these irregularities have become established by habit, it is very difficult to correct them—if it is not already too late to succeed in doing so[13].

---

12 ["Open Passage" or "Gazelle Passage"]
13 [These irregularities of the passage rhythm are frequently obvious in mod-

On the contrary, by beginning with the piaffe, it is easier to notice the irregularities in the diagonals and to correct them before they become permanent.

I propose to set forth the preparation and gradual perfecting of the piaffe, and then the development of the passage from the piaffe.

The program that I present seems to me, among [the different] ways of achieving the piaffe, the logical extension and complement of the training methods used by the majority of our military riders, most of whom I have been in a position to observe for many years.

---

ern competition horses trained to passage from the medium trot by way of repeated half-halts, resulting in one of the horse's diagonals slowing down or quickening its cadence more than the other one or just covering less ground than the other one.]

WHEN TO BEGIN THE TRAINING OF THE PIAFFE

The training for the piaffe should be commenced when the horse is completely schooled at the walk and trot.

It is essential that without a single alteration of the *mise en main,* the horse can execute the following:

1. Changes of length of stride in the trot and especially: the depart from a standstill to a trot, and the direct halt from a trot.

2. The work on two tracks[14], and in particular, the small volte at the trot with the haunches-in[15].

To help make matters clear I am adopting the following definitions:

MISE EN MAIN**[16] **(balance in the hand)—Absolute submission of the jaw in the *ramener* characterized by "its soft yielding... to the first request of the hand" (General L'Hotte).

RAMENER—A verticality of the head (or nearly vertical, position, possibly slightly beyond the vertical) *the poll always being the highest point of the head and neck.*

***DEMI-ARRÊT**[17]*—A firm upward movement [from bottom to top] on taut reins, with fingers well closed followed quickly by gradual relaxation of the fingers and giving with the hand.

This action is analogous to that of heaving up a heavy stone from the foot of a staircase and putting it gently down on one of the steps without damaging the surface of the step and without making any noise[18].

---

14   [shoulder-in, haunches-in and half-pass]
15   [travers on the *volte*]
16   "The *mise en main* or relaxation of the mouth in the *ramener* reduces tension for a moment to the degree of minimum contact."
Academic Equitation, General Decarpentry, Nicole Bartel translator, J.A.Allen, 1987
17   [French version of the half-halt that doesn't include any action of the seat or the legs unlike the German version of the same technique]
18   [This action is both upward and slightly forward, and is fundamentally different from the half-halt of La Guérinière: "to indicate a half-halt one holds the bridle hand close to one's body to retain and support the forehand of a horse that leans on his jaws, or when one wants to lower the horse's head [*ramener*] or to put him together [*rassembler*]" *Ecole de Cavalerie*, Xenophon Press, 2013]

HOW TO PREPARE FOR THE PIAFFE

Execute alternately, at first with fairly long intervals, the following two exercises:

1. From a standstill, depart to the trot, followed by a halt.

2. Halt from a trot, follow by a depart to the trot.

In the first of these exercises the number of steps between the depart and the halt is to be progressively reduced.

The measure of this reduction is always governed by the *mise en main*; the moment this alters, the horse is not yet supple enough to pass as quickly as desired from motion to a standstill and vice versa.

The reduction [of the interval] should therefore be made gradually.

In the second exercise, the length of time in the halt should also be shortened progressively[19].

The rider's ability to conserve the *mise en main* will indicate the relative ability to reduce the period of time required between the halt and the depart[20].

The trot should be rather slow, but definite and well-marked[21].

The halt and depart should be rigorously straight.

When the horse can execute, without losing the *mise en main*, each of these two exercises—a few steps at the trot and a halt of a few seconds,

19   [in order to create anticipation of the depart in the horse's mind]
20   [This requirement of Decarpentry focuses on the time it will take the rider to obtain perfect lightness to the hand through the relaxation of the neck, poll and mouth by either using vibrations or "*demi-arrêts*" during the immobility after the halt, or alternately, the pressure of the spurs near the girth as in the Captain Raabe method (the great model of Decarpentry for high school work).]
21   [meaning with enough energy to gain expressiveness, but not with so much that the trot becomes "passagey." That type of trot would create too slow a tempo, which would be opposite to the quickness of footfalls necessary in the early development of the first steps of piaffe.]

repeated five or six times in succession—the series should be finished with a longer trot followed by a prolonged halt, confirming the *mise en main*, by closing the fingers; and concluded with a long rest in place [at the halt] with the reins abandoned [resting] on the horse's neck[22].

During these exercises it is important to observe scrupulously the rule [of Baucher], "Hands without legs; legs without hands," which means:

Never increase the pressure of the hands and legs at the same time.

If the hand acts or increases its action, the leg should either maintain the intensity of its action or decrease it, as the case requires; but the leg should never increase its action while the hand is acting or increasing its action.

If the leg is active or increasing its action, the hand should remain passive or give, as the case requires.

The alternated contact of heel with flank and of hand with mouth should be effected at rapid enough intervals for the movements of hand and leg to follow one another smoothly, without interruption.

At the stage of dressage training which the horse should now have reached[23], the increases of the aids necessary to obtain the results wanted must be very slight, and the lessening of the passive aid generally serves no useful purpose; it is sufficient not to increase its intensity in direct and simultaneous opposition to the active aid.

If, however, the horse is going to sleep on his feet, push him forward with the leg while giving freely with the hand[24].

If the horse becomes heavy on the hand[25], *demi-arrêt* with cessation of the leg pressure at the same time.

Then begin again: leg active, hand fixed; hand active, leg fixed.

Avoid errors in [rider] position, especially, when the hand is active, that of leaning back too far with shoulders and chest, which would put an extra weight on the horse's haunches.

Keep the body vertical, with spurs, hips, and shoulders in line; put more weight on the stirrups and less in the seat when the horse's hindquarters diminish in their action.

---

22   [This is very important because the development of the horse's activity in preparation of the piaffe can eventually make the horse anxious, which can, in turn, lead to bracing. Interspersing long walks on a loose rein is also very helpful to maintain the horse's calm during that work.]
23   [before starting the study of piaffe and passage]
24   [the basic meaning of "legs without hands" to re-establish basic impulsion]
25   [We must go back immediately to the *demi-arrêt*, hand acting upward, not pulling, followed by instantaneous release.]

Avoid errors of the hand: passing too abruptly from activity to passivity, or vice versa. The extent of these movements should be strictly limited to what is necessary and should become imperceptible when the horse is ready to begin the piaffe[26].

Avoid similar errors of the leg.

---

26   [At this stage of training, the equilibrium of the piaffe is so fragile and the activity of the horse so tenuous, the slightest excess of unnecessary movement of the rider's body, or simple contraction of the legs, or of weight displacement from the rider, can "kill" the emerging mobility of the horse.]

HOW TO BEGIN THE PIAFFE

Alternate, as before, the action of the hand and of the leg, going from one to the other as soon as the first has begun to take effect and *before the effect is completed.*

As soon as the horse starts to move under the action of the leg, which relaxes immediately, restrain the horse's advancing with the hand *without stopping the movement.*

As soon as the horse tends to become immobile under the action of the hand, give instantly, and use the leg to prevent a complete cessation of the movement—and so on.

After a few alternating halts and departs, let the horse go forward freely by using an action of the rider's leg, and then, after a good trot, bring him to a definite halt with the hand and give him a long rest on the spot.

After a certain number of sessions the horse will begin to keep the cadence of the trot while scarcely advancing at each step.

Let him continue by himself for a few seconds, but take care to avoid letting him *stop* by himself; the exercise should always be concluded *at the command* of the rider, whether by halting or by going forward in a trot.

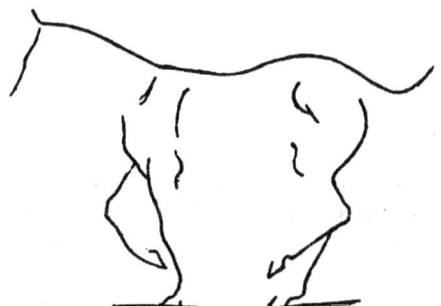

In the beginning piaffe, the overall attitude [of some horses] may appear consrained. The [horse's] vertebral column may not be sufficiently shortened[27], as it should be by the flexion of all of the hind leg joints. The ensemble of neck and trunk extends too far beyond in front and back, beyond the base

---

27   *raccourcie* [by the lack of forward tilting of the pelvis]

of support [horse's legs] which converge excessively under the body[28].

The upper part of the body can be contracted, and the loins[29] arched too much.

This can make the rider feel raised above the horse, his knees pushed up by the expansion of the ribs, which at the same time causes the flanks to draw in and seemingly shrink from contact with the rider's calves.

The contraction of the croup muscles can provoke a rather violent twitching of the tail.

The horse's hind legs are engaged too far forward, without sufficient flexion at the stifle and the hock.

The forelegs strike the ground too far back.

In each diagonal on the ground the horse's feet are too close together, making the base of support too short for him to trust himself on it for long, with the result that the legs are not raised enough and the alternating of the diagonals is often hurried[30].

The neck is generally too low and the angle at the poll too open. The mouth loses its suppleness, or, more often, nervously exaggerates its mobility.

---

28 [Decarpentry is referring to a potential excessive engagement of the hind legs of certain horses and the possible leaning and angling back of the front legs, with the front feet coming too far back under the body, the so-called "elephant on the drum."]

29 *le rein*

30 [The tempo can be lost in over-engaged horses because there is too much weight placed on the hind legs. On the other hand, horses who do not engage enough can have a slower tempo more akin to passage but with less collection as a result.]

DEVELOPING THE PIAFFE
See Plate I. Development of the Piaffe

When calm prevails in the trot *almost* on the spot, when the regularity of the beat is asserted, and when the twitching of the tail is subsiding[31], the rider should begin to modify the general posture of the horse by raising his head and neck in the *ramener* position.

RAISING THE NECK—This should be undertaken first, and continued gradually, until the end of the nose is almost level with the point of the haunches, while the *mise en main* and the *rassembler* remain constant.

As long as this result [the elevation of the neck] is only obtained under the *persistent* action of the hand, and ceases with it[32], it must be deemed inadequate[33].

Eventually, the horse should hold this position *of his own accord* and not seek to modify it before he is asked to do so[34].

The raising of the neck lessens by degrees the amount of advance at each step, often to the point that the horse will continue the movement on the spot.

If this result [movement in place] is not yet completely attained, the rider should not feel frustrated. Later on the work designed to raise the forelegs will achieve the reduction of the forward movement.

Usually, however, the horse tends to move slightly backward rather than to continue on the spot.

Unless the backward movement is unquestionably a sign of unwill-

---

31 [That is not the case with all horses and tail swishing, a sign of irritation and contraction, must be avoided as much as possible. The twisting of the tail can also be a reflex, as in horses with neuromuscular conditions such as shivers.]
32 [meaning that the horse lowers his head as soon as the hand doesn't hold him up]
33 [And further work with the lifting of the neck as described above remains necessary until the horse is strong enough to keep the position and maintain self-carriage thanks to sufficient flexion of the hind legs made comfortable by their progressive flexibility due to general gymnastics and the piaffe preparation.]
34 [in an extension of the neck for instance. "Long and Low" was not yet in fashion at the time and its benefits not recognized, as Oliveira did later (Beudant despised it). But even Captain Raabe already recommended the full horizontal extension of the neck following work in flexion.]

ingness bordering on defense[35], the horse should not be corrected with the spur; instead, he should be brought forward kindly with a measured and soft pressure of the leg, without any interruption of the rhythm. This should be repeated calmly each time he tries to find his balance by drawing back.

RAMENER—The vertical position of the head can only be maintained, when the neck is raised, by increased flexion at the poll.

When the position is obtained with perfect *mise en main*, that is; through *voluntary* obedience[36], it has a profound impact on the entire vertebral column and increases its supple flexion throughout[37].

The distance between the tip of the nose and tail is thus reduced and the body [head, neck and torso of the horse] overhangs the front and rear legs less. Moreover, the horse's legs each support closer to the weight-load of the *upper* extremities [the horse's torso][38]. The horse, therefore, while remaining collected, has his legs drawn less underneath him.

The back relaxes and flexes [upward], resulting in the haunches being lowered and the horse's pelvis being tucked [forward tilt] following the closure of the stifle and hock joints. The tail becomes still and rounded.

When the forelegs touch the ground they are almost in line vertically with the top of the withers; and similarly, the hind legs with the point of the haunches.

The horse's balance on each of the diagonals becomes steadier, since the base of support they give to the body is more in proportion to its length.

The horse gains confidence in the exercise and his steps become well spaced[39].

---

35 [meaning if it is a momentary loss of balance, or in fact a sign of excessive obedience to the request of ceasing forward motion]
36 [demonstrated by the horse gently mouthing the bit(s)]
37 [The flexion has an impulsive quality all its own and the horse who is brought to the perfect position of collection and left free to move in that position by the release of the rider's aids will suddenly gain a new level of energy that the rider did not even suspect was there.]
38 [Decarpentry means that the hips and shoulders are getting closer due to the collection of the horse, the "concentration of forces" toward the center of the horse.]
39 [The quieting down of the mind influences the relaxation of the topline (or vice versa) which in turn is responsible in great part for the improved general balance and the slower tempo of the movement.]

RAISING THE FORELEGS
See Plate I. Development of the Piaffe

When the horse has become calm and confident in this position, without altering either the *mise en main* or the cadence, and without trying to lower his neck or evade by changing the *ramener* position, the rider can begin to think about raising the forelegs, gradually bringing the forearms to the ideal position which is level with the point of the elbow.

This is achieved by putting weight on the foreleg that is on the ground and prolonging the standing time on this diagonal.

To keep his balance, the horse will lift the other foreleg and prolong the period of its suspension.

By putting pressure on the horse's neck with the right rein, for example, weight can be shifted to the left shoulder from the right [during the stance phase of the left front leg].

We can only achieve this result when the horse readily obeys the rein without evasion and commits himself confidently to its action.

This obedience is not usually obtained in the beginning piaffe training, and the horse's instinct causes him to evade the pressure by contracting in various ways, the most frequent of which are the following:

A. He more or less refuses to bend his neck in the direction demanded. The effect of the rein, instead of controlling the forehand as required, is transmitted down the spinal column to the left hind leg[40] and more or less paralyzes it.

The cadence is lost, first of all in the hindquarters[41].

B. He flexes his neck almost to the degree demanded, but does it by turning his head to the right.

The transfer of weight to the left sought by the rider is slight or not effected, since the right shoulder has not been sufficiently lightened.

The hindquarters, affected by the rein as before, again lose the rhythm, and the movement of the horse becomes more or less disturbed.

---

40 [by the general stiffness of the spine resulting from the contraction]
41 [and either the left hind or both hind feet become grounded]

C. He flexes his neck almost to the degree demanded, but does so by drawing his withers to the left. The left shoulder is then too far to the side for the left foreleg to stay in place, and that leg will move abruptly back under the shoulder. The cadence is lost, first in the forehand.

It is hardly possible to escape all these instinctive reactions in the training process, but it is of primary importance to avoid provoking a violent reaction. This can be achieved, up to a point, by the discretion of the requests of the hands, but above all by the OPPORTUNE TIMING of these requests.

Support on the right rein [sideways, to the left, against the right side of the horse's neck[42]] before the left foreleg touches the ground will move the placing of the left front to the left. And the result is the same if the pressure is continued until the leg is raised[43].

Therefore, the interval of time within which the effect of the rein can produce the desired result in an orderly way is very limited.

Moreover, the rider must possess perfect feeling for the lifting and lowering of the horse's feet which the *Écuyer* Aubert considered to be the basis of tact.

It is also necessary to develop the skill of balancing the horse between the different demands of the same rein; and no exercise is better for this preparation than alternating a shoulder-in with a half-pass, as described so precisely by Commandant de Salins in his two works known to all.[44]

In practice, it is therefore necessary:

1. Never to try to produce the effect of pressure on the rein when the horse is not perfect in the *mise en main*[45].

2. To give a prolonged squeeze by tightening the fingers on the right rein, with the right hand placed substantially above the withers, at the momoment when the left foreleg comes to the ground.

3. To rectify the problem little by little, and by small progressive attempts, the amount of pressure to give the right rein so that it will transport to the left shoulder ONLY the excess weight one wants it to support, without impairing the action of the hindquarters.

4. To increase little by little the intensity and duration of the tightening of the fingers, watching for the effect obtained [a slower cadence] so as to

---

42   *Tout effet d'appui de la rêne droite*

43   [This is an important action to correct horses who tend to land with their front feet too close together during the piaffe.]

44   J. de Salins, *Methode de dressage rapide du cheval de selle et d'obstacles*, Rennes: Oberthur, 1925, and *Secret de l'Art Équestre (Épaule en dedans)*, Rennes: Oberthur, 1931.

45   [Always insist on a completely relaxed connection as a preliminary condition and return to that preparation continuously.]

I. Development of the Piaffe

reduce the pressure of the fingers instantly if any disorder occurs[46].

It is of course very important that the results obtained are exactly equal for both shoulders. Nevertheless, in the beginning it is usually necessary to work on only one of them while the horse takes several steps [teaching one concept at a time to the horse]. One can even remain exercising one shoulder for some time [within the session].

As soon, however, as the rider obtains the slightest hint of lightness on one side, he should quickly seek the same result on the other. One shoulder may require more or less time than the other, but rarely do the two shoulders

---

46 [Failing to reduce the squeezing of the fingers when necessary may quicken his step and cause a nervous reaction instead of slowing it down as planned.]

take exactly the same duration of work. Horses, like human beings, are never naturally symmetrical[47].

Next, the rider should combine the two movements until the steps of the forelegs are exactly equal and made at a somewhat slower pace than at the start of the exercise[48].

Then begin working again on each shoulder separately [to correct any further unevenness].

During this entire period of work, the action of the hand should cease as soon as the horse's activity diminishes [loses impulsion]. The [rider's] leg should resume their action[49], without abruptness but firmly if need be[50], so that the diagonals definitely find their cadence [in case they have lost it].

[When the activity of the diagonals is restored], the leg can then relax and the action of the hand resumed[51].

---

47   [It is usually harder to place extra weight on the left shoulder and to remove weight off of the right shoulder for the majority of horses.]
48   [Evenness and slowness are the two parameters of cadence.]
49   [in a diagonal pattern: right leg with right hind lift and left hand with left shoulder lift, or replaced by a light touch of the whip]
50   [The strumming action of the spur or a soft, electric touch of the calf are probably the two best forms of aiding.]
51   [This follows the idea of Baucher—and Steinbrecht—repeated insistently by Decarpentry in this book on the fundamental separation of the aids to help the horse better understand the intentions and communication of the rider.]

DEVELOPING THE SCOPE OF THE MOVEMENT

It may happen that the knees bend past the right angle, bringing the front cannon bones behind the vertical when the forearms are raised close to the horizontal.

The piaffe then loses its correctness and grace.

The cause of this faulty action is that the *forehand is not sufficiently relieved of weight.* Bringing the cannon forward would destroy the forward equilibrium, and the horse is instinctively adverse to this danger.

If, in this faulty position, the horse is asked to raise his leg, he can only respond by throwing his foot toward the elbow without bringing it forward, and by exaggerated flexion of his knee.

This fault is often difficult to correct; yet it is relatively easy to avoid by not asking for elevation of the forelegs until the forehand is sufficiently lightened allowing the verticality of the front legs so that they are placed on the ground on a plumb-line directly beneath the top of the withers.

When this condition [verticality of the front leg on the ground] has not been achieved, and the forelegs have begun a cramped action[52], no further attempt should be made to raise them. One should recommence the exercise at the point where the unfortunate *over-flexion* began.

Usually the lack of lightness in the forehand is not caused by an insufficiently raised neck, but rather by a lack in the *ramener* and the *mise en main*.

It may well be that this insufficiency in the lightness in the *ramener* position escaped the notice of the rider well in advance of his attempt at the

---

52 [referring to a movement of the front legs in which the elbows of the horse do not move freely forward and stay too close to the girth area]

piaffe, and was already evident in the work at the trot, at the walk, and even at the halt.

One should therefore go back in the training program as far as needed to remedy the error at the point where it began to appear, and to obtain a better stability in the *ramener* with the *mise en main* in all the work that follows, up to the point where the exercise of raising the forelegs in the piaffe may be undertaken.

It should be also noted that the drawing back of the cannons often coincides with a tendency to back up [in the piaffe].

This should be corrected by requiring a slight but well-marked advance of the front legs at each step.

Part 2: Development of the Piaffe

I.

RECTIFYING THE GENERAL POSITION BY RAISING THE FOREHAND

I. — ACTION OF THE HAND

When asked to raise his head and neck, the horse resists (note the slant of the shanks of the bit in the photograph I).

The horse is high in the croup (observe [pofile] the [relative height of the] point of the croup above the joint of hip [compared with the later photographs]). The point of the buttocks, the stifle, the hock, and the knee are hardly bent. The horse is tilted forward on his left foreleg, which is placed too far back, whereas his right foreleg is barely off the ground.

The rider is lifted up by the contraction of the back (a horizontal line from the tip of the ears goes through the rider's chest pockets). His knees are also lifted and his legs are spread and pushed forward by the swelling of the chest (note the distance from the rider's knee to the edge of the saddle, and from his foot to the girth)[53].

---

53   [We may be much more appreciative of the horse raising his back today as a desirable outcome, but in this case, the back is raised by an effect of the undesirable lifting of the croup.]

II.

II. — USE OF THE HAND

The horse yields to the hand (see the minimal slant of the shanks of the bit compared to the previous picture). His back flexes (see the lowered position of the rider: the horizontal line from the tip of the ears passes above the rider's shoulder)[54]. The horse's chest deflates (see the distance from rider's knee to edge of saddle, and from his foot to the girth). The haunches are lowered (the point of the croup has disappeared; the flexion of the hindquarter joints is emphasized, as is the elevation of the suspended hind leg[55]).

The forehand is tipped forward less (see the distance of the vertical from end of nose to tip of forefoot on ground). The forefoot in suspension leaves the ground with greater freedom. The flexion of the knee is increased.

The rider is sitting into the horse, and his legs are in the proper position.

---

54   [The rider is not pushed up by a forcefully lifted croup in this photograph.]
55   [both hind legs are flexed more, one up and one down]

III.

DEVELOPING THE ACTION
OF THE FORELEGS

III. — USING THE HAND
(up and down and from right to left, to lighten the right shoulder)

There is resistance in the back, and the chest swells. The forehand gives a little, the neck swings to the right and draws back. The bent position of the foreleg on the ground shows that it is still too far back to permit a durable balance. The right foreleg is lightened and lifted, and the knee is almost on a vertical line with the ears. Because the spine is contracted, the movement of the left hind leg is affected by the rein and reduced in action.

The rider is stiff, his torso tips back, and his legs go forward.

IV.

IV. — YIELDING OF THE HAND AND USE OF THE LEG
to activate the hind legs of the horse

The back yields and the rider sits into the saddle. The croup is lowered and the joints of the hind legs flex. The foreleg on the ground is almost vertical and has advanced closer to its proper position. The right foreleg is visibly lifted (the action as shown, however, is exaggerated because the photograph was not taken in full profile).

V.

V. — FIXITY of the hand and leg to let the horse
find his own equilibrium [balance].

Here, the horse is approaching his proper balance, as the improvement in his general position testifies, but he has not quite found it, as can be seen by his opened jaw[56].

He is still too high in the croup. The hind leg on the ground is well placed but insufficiently flexed; neither is the hind leg off the ground sufficiently flexed, especially at the hock, with the result that the fetlock joint is not far enough under the mass above it, nor is the foot sufficiently raised.

The foreleg on the ground is well placed (the vertical from the toe reaches the upper third of the neck).

The foreleg off the ground is correct.

The torso of the rider is too far back, which adds weight to the hind leg off the ground[57].

---

56 [a mark of effort and slight nervousness]
57 [Decarpentry is very severe on critiquing his own, admirable performance.]

Part 3: The Passage

THE PASSAGE

To pass from the piaffe to the passage, obtained through the program which has just been described, one should reduce the barrier of opposition effected by the rider's hand on the thrust of the horse's hind legs in order to transform a portion of their energy into a forward movement, which was previously directed solely up and down in the piaffe.

In general, the yielding of the hand will cause, at first, a marked hesitation in the horse, which must be overcome with an action of the leg, used frankly but with moderation and without abruptness.

The horse, responding to this signal [the action of the rider's legs described above], loses his balance forward and [usually] passes into an ordinary trot [as expected] after two or three somewhat rhythmic steps.

For the first few days it is desirable to let him trot freely some tens of meters without opposition of the hand, then bring him to a halt and reward him.

Then, one should continue as before, but seeking the *mise en main* as soon as the forward movement is established, and finish with a halt with *mise en main*.

When the horse can halt easily while keeping his *mise en main*, he is to be brought to a halt as soon as the several steps of CADENCED trot following the piaffe degenerate into an ordinary trot[58].

Finally, one passes from the piaffe into the cadenced trot, halts as soon as the cadence is lost, one calls for the piaffe [again], one restarts again into the cadenced trot, and so on, until the cadenced trot is easily maintained with the horse in the *mise en main* without rushing the beats, by advancing frankly and slowly.

One must be especially careful in the beginning not to start out from the horse's "maximum" piaffe, but on the contrary, from a less elevated piaffe that is well defined and above all perfectly calm.

Going from the piaffe to the cadenced trot demands, at least at first, an extra effort of the hind legs.

If the elevation of the piaffe has already demanded the maximum ef-

---

58   [or possibly before, so the rider must try to guess the changing capability of the horse and stop before the horse quits. By using this approach, the horse starts to wait for the request of the rider and eventually keeps on going in the new cadence he just learned until asked to stop.]

fort, the horse will "fall" into a trot with no cadence instead of "throwing" himself into an energetic cadenced trot.

Little by little the horse acquires skill in this exercise, and in large measure substitutes for the extra effort of the hind legs a new balance of his body which transforms part of the execution of vertical movement of the piaffe into forward movement.

One can eventually start from a more elevated piaffe, but always taking care to not let the cadence be extinguished with the development of the forward movement.

One must not progress to start from a more elevated piaffe unless the cadence of the preceding movement [piaffe] was fully maintained in the forward movement [the passage].

The cadenced trot is thus transformed little by little into the passage.

GOING TO PASSAGE FROM PIAFFE

I.

An even piaffe, but of a less elevated development than the horse is capable. This is a favorable piaffe from which one can acquire an energetic passage at the beginning [of training this movement].[59]

---

59 [This is a very important principle of dressage: not to use maximum power before a transition into a new movement, or the horse may falter in the change to passage because he may not have reserves of energy left to use in the transition.]

II.

Overuse of the leg. The horse loses his balance forward and throws himself onto the rider's hand. In spite of this fault, the "form" of the passage is satisfactory.

The photograph, taken at an angle, exaggerates the gesture of the hind legs and diminishes that of the forelegs.

[As a result] the rider is left [behind] surprised by the inertia; his torso is too far back.

III.

Use of the hand to restore the equilibrium (by alternating the actions of both reins).

The visible resistance of the horse's mouth corresponds to the faulty engagement of the hind leg on the ground. The legs in suspension are correct. The rider's heels are in the air [unfortunately, but] the position of his torso is better than in the preceding photograph.

IV.

The resistance to the hand has diminished, the hind leg on the ground has come forward, but the croup is too high and the loins are sunken. The foreleg on the ground is placed too far forward.

The rider's heels are even higher in the air; his torso, which is behind the movement, is thrown back and contributes to the widening of the loins.

V.

The resistance has diminished even more; it has not ceased, however, as is shown by the slant of the bit and the opened jaw.

The [horse's] general posture is better. The *ramener* and the flexion of the loins are almost correct. The hind leg on the ground is still not sufficiently advanced under the mass above it and is insufficiently flexed. On the other hand, the suspended hind leg is flexed and lifted too much, doubtless from the request of a spur too far back and too high. The foreleg on the ground is well placed, but the foreleg off the ground is not raised enough and is not flexed enough at the knee.

The rider is very badly placed, sitting too far back with his torso behind the movement and his knees and heels up.

I.

The horse is in his natural trot, without being collected. Through a natural defect [of conformation] his hind legs always have a higher action than his forelegs[60] when the rider does not intervene to modify this obvious imperfection of gait.

---

60   [a problem inherent to the downhill build of this Thoroughbred]

PASSAGE OBTAINED FROM THE TROT

The passage developed from the trot often has a more extended style than that developed from the piaffe, even with a horse that has been schooled first in the piaffe; but it is then easier to modify the style and bring it closer to the classic manner.

II.

The *mise en main* modifies this difference in elevation, but since it is done with the hand too low, it is insufficient to correct the difference in elevation.[61]

---

61 [i.e., Correct the hind leg from lifting higher than the diagonal front]

III.

The correction[62] is obtained by lowering the hind legs and not, as it should be, by raising the forelegs.[63]

---

62 [correction of lowering the height of the raised hind leg relative to the height of the raised front leg shown in the previous photograph II]

63 [Decarpentry doesn't tell us how he achieves this goal, but we can assume that it is through a combined action of seat and legs. He obviously prefers to elevate the front end in order to lower the back end.]

IV.

The foreleg is raised but the hind leg on the ground is not sufficiently engaged, with the result that the *mise en main* and the *ramener* are lost[64].

---

64 [through the hollowing and tension of the back accompanied by the swishing of the tail]

V.

This passage is nearing, yet not attaining, the classic style. The general position of the horse is correct but the foreleg is not raised sufficiently, a fault further emphasized by the photograph, which was not taken in full profile. The rider, however, benefits from the camera angle, which gives the impression that his position is relatively correct[65].

---

65   [In final analysis, the passage obtained by Decarpentry from piaffe looks a lot better than the version he obtained from the regular trot, but we do not have the benefit of video to get a fuller impression of Professeur's performance. Decarpentry combined both methods to work on transitions both from piaffe and from trot as a way to complete the training of his horse.]

BIBLIOGRAPHICAL NOTE

Aside from J. de Salins, whom the author cites on page 86, writers on equitation named in the preface and text of *Piaffer and Passage*, in the order of their mention, and their principal works, are:

Count d'Aure (1799-1863)
Traite d'équitation, 1834; revised, 1844, 1870
Cours d'équitation, 1850 rev. 1852, 1853

François Baucher (1796-1873)
Dictionnaire raisonné d'équitation, 1833, rev. 1851
Dialogues sur l'équitation, 1834
Methode d'équitation, basée sur de nouveaux principes, 1842, rev. 1859

General Decarpentry (1878-1956)
Academic Equitation, 1987

James Fillis (1834-1913)
Principes de dressage et d'équitation, 1890, rev. 1892
Journal de dressage, 1903

Captain J.-F.-M.-J. de Saint-Phalle (1867-1908)
Dressage et emploi du cheval de selle, 1899, rev. 1904
Equitation, 1907

General A.-F. L'Hotte (1825-1904)
Un Officier de cavalerie—Souvenirs de Général L'Hotte, 1905
Questions équestres, 1906

P.-A. Aubert (ca. 1783-1863)
Traité raisonné d'équitation, 1836

J. de Salins
Methode de dressage rapide du cheval de selle et d'obstacles,
    Rennes: Oberthur, 1925
Secret de l'Art Équestre (Épaule en dedans), Rennes: Oberthur, 1931.

General Decarpentry

"All along his life and since his early childhood, while always doing his duty as a military officer in peace time as well as during the two World Wars, he has passionately studied everything related to the equestrian sport. But it was the Academic equitation that mourns his loss in 1956 as one of its greatest masters and scholars. According to his friend and occasional student the Colonel Lesage (Chief *Écuyer* of the School of Saumur), he was a remarkable *écuyer* with an astonishing equestrian cuture, having studied in depth everything that had been written on the subject since Herodotus."
-Colonel Henry Challan Belval in "*L'Annee Hippique*", 1956.

The preparation for the writing of *Piaffe and Passage* consists of a lifetime of dedication to dressage, a dedication rooted in the traditional values of the old school of equitation and directed to the search for the understanding of the art of riding.

Born in 1878, Decarpentry came from a family of horsemen. His grandfather Eugene Caron was a pupil of Baucher. His great-uncle François Caron, the chief riding master of the Tsar of Russia, was proclaimed by Fillis to be his model. Edouard Caron, his uncle, owned a school of equitation and was the first to put the young Decarpentry in the saddle. It is not surprising that Decarpentry had a vocation to dressage like his family, and chose a military career in the French cavalry.

For twenty years as a member of the Cadre Bleu and the Cadre Noir, eight of them in the capacity of *écuyer* at Saumur, Decarpentry was engaged in the study of d'Aure, Baucher, L'Hotte and the many other masters to whose wealth of equestrian writings he fell heir. In the examination of the theories [he read the classics] and the practical experience afforded by trial and error during daily riding, Decarpentry not only produced beautifully schooled horses but developed and put into writing the framework of a logical and methodical program of dressage as a guideline for others.

In 1947 Decarpentry became the President of the Dressage Commission of the *Federation Equestre Internationale* [F.E.I.][66]. He undertook the

---

66 [He was President of the jury of the dressage competitions at the London Olympics. His presence was very much sought after everywhere in Europe where his technical authority and unquestionable competence gave him a very special

difficult task of setting the standard for international dressage competitions and adjusting their requirements to a correct form acceptable by all. He also had the delicate mission of bringing strong national equestrian opinions into harmony. His success on the juries resulted in reconciling many differences of equestrian thought and, at the same time, in creating a universal ideal for the perfect dressage horse[67].

Drawing upon his vast knowledge of the literature and the wisdom of his practical experience, Decarpentry presents the fruit of his labor in six works which, in turn, place him among the great masters whom he followed so faithfully, and so modestly.

---

position amongst international experts. (Challan Belval, already cited)]

67 [He spoke German fluently and was a close friend of Dr. Gustav Rau and General von Holzing-Berstett (president of the F.E.I.) with whom he worked tirelessly to harmonize the judging system. He was reputed to have demonstrated a complete absence of nationalism as an international judge. Decarpentry was the first to transform a vast array of dressage ideas expressed by individual authors into a corpus of definitions we now take for granted as the universally accepted rules of the F.E.I..

Here is a noted example of the nationalistic dressage concepts Decarpentry had to deal with. After explaining the origin of repeated flying changes of Baucher, he makes the following analysis in a letter to General Wattel, the most brilliant Chief Rider of Saumur (creating many implications for the equilibrium of the piaffe).

"I believe that the equilibrium of the Old School, with horses really sitting, makes the flying change very difficult and the one-tempi changes practically impossible. On the other hand, the horizontal balance devised by Baucher makes the tempi easy, and they might even be easier with a horse on the forehand."

Follow a series of examples.

"Conclusion: riders using horizontal balance, or even on the forehand (French and French admirers) want one tempi changes in international classes. To oppose them as a form of reprisals, the Swedes, Swiss and other Germanophiles demand a movement that can only be done in a very sitting position: very tight counter changes in canter," etc.

On the other hand, he had great admiration for certain German trainers: "Stensbeck {Oskar Maria Stensbeck 1858-1939, trained dressage horses, became a civilian head groom of the cavalry riding school in Hannover, founded the "Stensbeck Riding College," and became one of the most important riding instructors. At the age of 72, he wrote down his experiences in a book called *Reiten*.} who is more than 70 years old, rides everyday at the School [of Hannover] where he has no official functions. I have seen him work. He is a prince [on a horse]."

-Letter of Decarpentry to Colonel Lesage, 1937.]

Here are the titles of his works[68]:

Piaffer et Passage, 1932
[*The Spanish Riding School in Vienna Piaffe and Passage*, Xenophon Press, 2013]

L'Ecole espagnole de Vienne 1948
[*The Spanish Riding School in Vienna Piaffe and Passage*, Xenophon Press, 2013]

Baucher et son école, 1948
[*Baucher and His School*, Xenophon Press, 2011]

Equitation académique, 1949
[Academic Equitation, J. A. Allen, 1971, 1987]

Les Maitres écuyers du manège de Saumur, de 1814 a 1874, 1954

L'Essentiel de la Méthode de haute école de Raabe, 1958

---

68 [These books are indispensable reading for everyone interested in the evolution of dressage in the 19th and 20th centuries. The practice of dressage cannot evolve completely without a reasonable knowledge of our equestrian culture and the reading of Decarpentry's books is an unavoidable part of this curriculum.]

www.ingramcontent.com/pod-product-compliance
Lightning Source LLC
Chambersburg PA
CBHW060515300426
44112CB00017B/2677